Motor Oil
for a
Car Guy's Soul

ISBN 0-9729445-2-4

Published by River's Bend Press Inc.,
PO Box 606, Stillwater, Minnesota, 55082 USA
Visit our website at www.riversbendpress.com

First trade paperback edition 2004
Cover design by Peterson Design
Layout and interior design by Peterson Design [petersondesign@mn.rr.com]
Illustrations by Daniel Belic [ultimatebabies@hotmail.com]
H. Jackson Photo courtesy of University of Vermont
Edited by Wm. Schmaltz

Library of Congress Cataloging-in-Publication Data

Clemens, Kevin, 1957-
Motor oil for a car guy's soul / Kevin Clemens.
p. cm.
"These essays were originally published in European Car magazine"—T.p. verso.
ISBN 0-9729445-2-4
1. Automobiles—Popular works. 2. Clemens, Kevin, 1957—-Anecdotes. 3. Automobile engineers—United States—Anecdotes. I. Title.
TL146.5.C565 2004
629.222—dc22
2004015158

For my parents

TABLE OF CONTENTS

FOREWORD

As the editor of an automotive enthusiast magazine, I've met plenty of nutty car guys...and there's not one of them any nuttier than Kevin Clemens. Don't misunderstand. Kevin is nutty like a fox is crazy, as he's one of the few people I know who have managed to turn their boyhood passion into a rich professional life. The young boy who helped his father rebuild the family's Borgward station wagon grew up to become an engineer, journalist and amateur racer, living the life of a car guy and getting paid for it!

I first met Kevin when he was the engineer in charge of the press launch of a new high-performance tire and I listened as he described the complex kinematics of BMW's multi-link rear axle. Accompanied by articulate swoops and flutters of his hands, he drew a clear and concise picture that even thick-skulled automotive editors could understand. I was impressed and we struck up a friendship. Little did I know that this highly intelligible egghead would someday become one of *my* magazine's most valued contributors. His monthly "On The Line" column is a mainstay of *European Car*, giving the magazine a dollop of Kevin's quintessential car guy personality.

It's always an adventure to read Kevin's columns. I never know what's coming next. He admits that his point of view ranges from cranky to joyous, hopeful to cynical, but he's always got something to say. One month he'll write about a mid-pack session at the wheel of a Lotus racecar, and the next month about his around-the-world drive in a 1959 Mercedes-Benz sedan. He can intelligently describe the strengths and weaknesses of the most intricate engineering of today's ultra-sophisticated automobiles, while reveling in clever designs from the dawn of the horseless carriage.

The breadth and depth of Kevin's car guy-ness can be summed up by some of the cars he's owned. The first was a 1958 Berkeley with a 328cc Excelsior engine, which he acquired by trading two of his short wave radios. That car was eventually traded for an MG Midget and then a Ford Capri rally car, various Austin-Healeys, more MGs, a few Bugeyes and a smattering of Saabs. He has had more sports cars than most people have fingers and toes. He has owned a series of slow, yet charismatic, racing cars, many of which form the fodder for his more memorable tales. I could go on, but he adds or subtracts cars from his stable so quickly that any list of what he has now would surely be out of date before it reached the presses.

It's too bad we can't all meet some Saturday morning in Kevin's gearhead-heaven garage and trade lies. Somehow you just know before long we would all be gathered around an example of some arcane automotive trivia, discussing its place in history and coming to the realization that it was built by car nuts just like us. In this book, however, you're now holding the next-best way to share his adventures, his great storehouse of automotive lore and the wisdom of a lifelong car guy.

Greg N. Brown
Editor, *European Car*

PREFACE

I used to have a real job. For the first ten years of my professional life after college, I was a design engineer for one of the world's largest tire companies. It's hard to imagine a better job for an automotive enthusiast, as I was responsible for the development of both high performance and racing tires in North America. It was fun, but when the opportunity to become an automotive journalist was presented to me, I jumped ship. The life of an automotive journalist is much better than having a real job. You get to travel to faraway places, drive amazing cars, stay in fabulous hotels, eat wonderful meals, meet interesting people and you get paid to write a story about it all. You'll never get rich being an automotive journalist, but you sure can live as though you are. If you do it right, you can find yourself hammering across the Taklamakan Desert in China, negotiating a rutted trail in the high Andes or sliding an early MG around some of the most famous race tracks in America.

After several years as the Technical Editor at *Automobile Magazine,* Greg Brown from *European Car* asked me if I would write a column for his magazine. The magazine's Managing Editor, Sherri Collins, said they wanted me to add some "personality" to *European Car.* We called the column "On the Line."

I like old cars, but I also like new ones. I like history, technology, nostalgia, bravery, adventure, and irony. I try to write about these things, not just for myself, but also for a new generation of auto enthusiasts who have never heard of William Lyons, nor know what a Bugatti looks like. In the fifties and sixties, automotive journalist Ken Purdy was that writer for a generation of car enthusiasts. Sports cars were new to the American scene and Purdy, among a small number of others, put a voice to that movement. He helped many of us learn how we were supposed to feel and act when in the presence of automotive greatness. And while it is absolutely true that the automobiles, pickup trucks, minivans and SUVs of today are better in almost every way than the cars of the past, it is old cars that keep us fascinated. If I could wish anything it would be that the columns I have written evince a small amount of the style and grace that Ken Purdy had in his books.

I learned about cars the old-fashioned way. My father helped me figure out how to change spark plugs, adjust ignition points and get a carburetor to work. Today it's mostly middle-aged and older car guys who know how to do these things. That isn't to say that a twenty-something car guy who has never had these experiences can't be a car guy, it's just that the route might be slightly different, since modern vehicles don't have ignition points and carburetors. (By the way, I am using the term "Car Guy" in a completely non-gender specific and politically correct way. I know lots of women who are "Car Guys" and would be really angry if you called them otherwise.) What I am trying to do in these essays is bridge the gap between young and old, and make sure we don't forget where we come from, and let car guys of all ages know that an automotive adventure lies around every corner. The thing about adventures is that they don't come looking for you, you have to go and find them; and they aren't always fun, but always prove entertaining.

I hope you enjoy this collection of some of my best "On the Line" columns. I've tried to create a book that would be fun and exciting, nostalgic, helpful, inspiring and even surprising to read. So sit down, buckle up and enjoy the ride.

Kevin Clemens
Lake Elmo, Minnesota
June, 2004

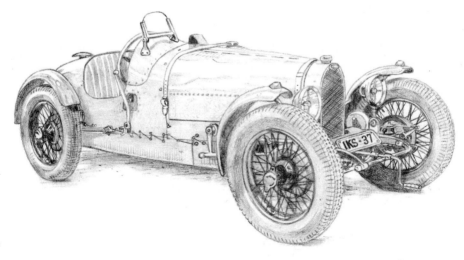

1927 Bugatti - Type 37

CHAPTER 1

First Time Charmers

The first car I ever drove was a white 1965 Opel Kadette Coupe Z. "Drove" might be too strong a term, for my initial motoring experience was being pulled around a deserted subdivision by a long rope attached to a Mercury station wagon. My father had purchased the Kadette as cheap transportation for my elder sister to take her to and from two years of Junior College. But first, we had to get it running and that entailed a new set of main bearings. The problem was that General Motors entrusted the sales and service of American Opels to Buick dealers. In the early seventies your average Buick dealer had about as much use for an Opel as they did any other small import car, which is to say none. They were even less interested in selling parts.

My father, ever resourceful, managed to convince them to order a set of main bearings for the tiny 993cc four-cylinder engine that lurked under the hood of the boxy little coupe. A few weeks later the bearings arrived and after a weekend's work under the hot Florida sun, the engine was apart and back together, ready to serve my sister's very basic transportation needs. Except—the engine wouldn't start. Not only would it not start, it wouldn't even turn under the motivation of the starter motor. A jump to the battery only produced wisps of smoke from the starter as it gamely tried to turn over the tightly bound engine. It seems that Buick, in their limited

Opel wisdom, had sent us oversized bearings, ones that were thicker than the usual standard bearings. This left us with a crankshaft that was firmly held in place by its very own set of main bearings.

My father's solution was a simple one. He would drive the family station wagon around the neighborhood, towing the Opel on a rope with me driving. *Me driving?* Up until that time I had been allowed to occasionally, and very carefully, back the Mercury down the driveway. At fourteen, this was more than I could have ever hoped for! Patiently, the mysteries of the flat-tow were explained to me: Keep tension in the rope by using the brakes. Keep an eye on the rope and don't let it get caught on either vehicle in a turn. Signal with your hands for stop or go. We carefully we tied the rope between the two vehicles. Another step-forward in my automotive education was about to begin.

Getting to an unfinished housing project was uneventful, but it did seem to require every ounce of attention from my overloaded brain cells. The next phase required even more from me. Until now I had been in neutral, using only the brake pedal. This next phase was different. My father would bring the Mercury up to about 20-mph, while I, still piloting the powerless Opel, would let out the clutch in second gear, with the ignition turned off. Crude? Perhaps, but we saw it as a quick way to grind down the oversized bearings and get the engine running.

For most of the afternoon we drove around and around the paved roads of that unfinished subdivision the big V-8 in the station wagon straining slightly as it towed the poor little Opel around each block. Every few miles we would stop and try the starter motor. At first there was no significant result. But, gradually, we could sense that things were turning easier. As the afternoon wore on, we began to ponder a new strategy. If the engine was turning over, why not help it by turning on the ignition? A few more passes and a few more hits with the starter and we decided it was time. This time I switched on the ignition before popping the clutch in second. With a backfire, the little motor growled to life. I was able to slacken the towrope by pressing slightly on the gas pedal. *I was driving!* A whole world began to open before my eyes. We rolled to a stop and I pressed in the clutch and the engine immediately fell silent. The bearings were still too tight to allow the little engine to run on its own. But for a very brief instant, I had driven a vehicle, not a go-kart, but a real vehicle under its own power. More laps the next day and we could get it to idle. Another day and we had a usable and happy little car.

My sister used the car for two years, treating it as the transportation appliance that it was. But for me, (having recently discovered the sport of rallying, through the pages of car magazines), it was a factory car ready to join the team of Opel Kadettes that were contesting the World Rally Championship. Eventually, I got my license and that little white Opel taught me tons about understeer and the decided limitations of a transverse leaf spring front suspension. When my sister went off to college, the Opel was traded on a 1965 Mustang, a better car for her in many respects, but not as important as that Opel was to me.

My daughter turned thirteen. In the middle of the summer, early on a Sunday morning, she and I went to a deserted mall parking lot with my 1952 MG TD. I drove to a level spot in the parking lot and pulled on the handbrake. I climbed out and walked over to her side of the low slung little roadster. "Your turn," I said, motioning to the large, cord-wrapped steering wheel. Her mouth opened and her eyes nearly popped as she climbed out and walked around to the other side of the idling sports car. I explained the clutch and the brake and that I could kill the ignition and pull the handbrake if anything went seriously wrong. Jessica listened brightly, but two problems were immediately apparent. It was difficult for her to reach the pedals and if she scooted forward to reach them, she had trouble seeing over the scuttle. Oh well, I should have brought a pillow. Still, we didn't let minor setbacks stop us and she revved the eager little engine and slipped the clutch. We lurched away and she started her first tentative laps, driving around the parking lot.

Her experiences until then, like mine at her age, were on bicycles and go-karts, so it took her a while to get used to the amount of steering that was needed to negotiate a bend. I made her start and stop a few times to get the feel of the clutch. Sometimes she was smooth, other times jerky. So much to learn. Finally, when I sensed overload, I suggested we switch seats and head for home. On the way I showed her how I was shifting and how I could leave from a standing start smoothly.

Then I explained the story of that little white Opel to her and how important it was to me that the very first car she drove be a significant one. Something beyond the ordinary. She smiled and nodded thoughtfully. I only hope my old MG becomes as important to her as that silly white Opel is to me.

CHAPTER 2

The Red Car: An old book, a simpler time

It was red, fire-engine red. It was low, as Steve's MG was low, but it had none of the chunky look of the yellow car outside. This one was lean and racy and angular, with fenders that made no attempt to curve or blur into the body lines, but stood out in a clean sharp sweep over the wheels.

The wheels were enormous; they were almost ludicrous at first glance. They were gleaming silvery wire wheels, standing high and narrow with the rakish scarlet body of the car slung low between them, looking even now as though it were crouched close to the ground, ready to spring forward. The car looked almost alive. It had a personality all its own— an arrogant, insolent, challenging way of looking you right in the eye and saying 'Drop dead!'

The above passage is from a slim paperback novel called *The Red Car*. It was written by Don Stanford and published by Scholastic Book Services in 1954. The car he is talking about is a 1948 MG TC roadster that Stanford's main character, sixteen year-old Happy "Hap" Adams, is seeing for the first time. The car has been heavily wrecked by having been driven off a mountain road and young Hap hatches a wild scheme to bring the little sports car back to life. There are cer-

5

1949 MG TC

tain defining moments when you are growing up. Events that shape your life and your future. For me, it was finding a copy of *The Red Car* at the public library when I was twelve years old.

Don Stanford was a magazine writer in the 1950s. He lived in Norfolk, Connecticut and was also an amateur racer. His experiences while racing in Colorado led him to set *The Red Car* there. Although Stanford had already written stories and serialized novels for *True* magazine and others, *The Red Car* was his first novel specifically written for a younger audience. The book was quite popular in its time and had its fifth printing in 1965.

The story is straightforward, filled with references to the importance of truth and respect for parents. This was the 1950s, after all. But, beyond all of the admirable values and lessons learned by Hap Adams, is a kind of blueprint of how to be a sports car enthusiast of the first order. When the book first came out, this was important. Sports cars were still relatively new to American highways and it is clear that Stanford wanted to convert as many young people to the cause as he possibly could. He explained why these cars are the way they are:

> *The little car rode hard: there didn't seem to be any springs under it at all. It bounced and jarred and danced over the road; but it was instantly responsive to the slightest touch on the steering wheel— and Hap could see that it wouldn't be, if it were floating along on mushy comfortable springs, there would be too much sway, too much give in the spring to compensate for. Comfort in this case, was well-sacrificed to precision; the car felt sensitive and spirited, but you felt you could really depend on it.*

To explain the intricacies of sports car driving and racing, Stanford invented the character of Phillippe "Frenchy" Lascelle, a

French nobleman and racer who had moved to the United States under mysterious circumstances and opened a garage in Hap Adam's hometown. Frenchy helps Hap repair and rebuild the wrecked MG and then teaches him how to drive a sports car.

> *He tapped the big dial of the tachometer with a finger, and the gesture seemed to remind him that Hap was beside him. He turned, his eyes were alive again; he said with emphasis, tapping the dial of the tachometer: 'It is with this instrument one drives this car, Happy, not with the speedometer, there. When you have a little engine, a good engine but an engine that is not big, you must learn where is her best power, and you must drive her there, eh?*
>
> *An engine has a power curve, Happy: when she goes slow she must fight to turn herself over before she can do anything else, before she can work for a car. When she goes a little faster her momentum helps her to turn herself over; then more of her power can work for you. But when she goes too fast, she is not efficient anymore, the curve comes down again. And there is a point she will break, if she goes too fast.*
>
> *You must learn to know your engine, Happy. You must find the peak of her power curve, the speed where she is happiest working for you, where she delivers the most power. And there you must drive her, always. To change speeds you have gears; you do not put such a car as this one in the wrong gear and simply use the engine to make her go faster or slower. She does not have the extra power; she has only what she needs. But she has all she needs!'*

To a twelve-year old, these words were like some sort of secret magical code. To learn them promised entrance into a secret society. One filled with exotic racy cars and seductive women. Yes, Stanford also had several women's roles in his novel, somewhat stereotypical, as this was the fifties, but at least women weren't excluded from this view of sports car heaven.

The mid-fifties were a time of controversy in American sports car racing as the concept of amateur versus professional drivers was at the forefront. Stanford doesn't shy away from the subject and creates a road-race in the streets of Hap's hometown to strongly favor the idea of gentleman amateur drivers:

> *'There isn't any rule against that, no,' Les Bailey answered, and now there was cold dislike in his voice, 'although we'd've made one if we'd known your friend was a hotshoe professional driver. This isn't that kind of a race, Mister. This is a quiet little get-together for amateurs; for novices, mostly. It isn't a Grand Prix, and it isn't for blood, and it isn't for the record. There aren't even any trophies, to amount to anything; this one is for fun. And I don't think John Arata drives for fun! How'd you do at LeMans last year? How about the Carrera PanAmericana, the Mexican Road Race?' 'Not bad both times,' Arata said, sneering. 'And you forget, kid. I can drive professional out of the country, if you're going to bring that up, and it doesn't affect my amateur standing in the U.S.A.'*

This was pretty heady stuff for a kid's book about sports cars and it was hard to read it without feeling like you were being drawn into a battle of amateurs-against-professionals that had already been fought and lost by the time I read *The Red Car* at the end of the sixties.

I recently found a copy of *The Red Car* over the internet. It was in a used bookshop in California and the price was $3.00. Reading it now, as an adult, I expected to find it childish and simplistic. But once again, as it happened thirty years before, I was drawn into a world of sports cars and gentlemanly driving that only exists today in the memories of those who took part in these earliest days of the sports car movement. Maybe it's not a definitive history, nor great literature. But this slim book captures the spirit of the time, a spirit that many are trying to recapture at vintage race meetings around the country. It should be required reading for everyone who likes old sports cars, no matter what their age.

Don Stanford dedicated *The Red Car* to his son. The inscription sums up the entire early sports car era as well as anything written in the period: *"To Donald K. Stanford, Jr. and to other boys of all ages who admire fine cars and good sportsmanship."*

CHAPTER 3

The Thousand Dollar Car: A beater for all seasons

A few years ago we moved from our rural Virginia mountain retreat to the hustle and bustle of Columbus, Ohio. Moving from five acres in the country to the heart of a city with a million-plus population required some adjustment. Traffic shuttled past our downtown Victorian home at every hour of the day and night and parking was at a premium. City dwellers adopt a parking–by-Braille approach that they never taught us in Driver's Ed, and when it snows, the plow trucks dump salt on the roads to make the snow melt quickly. With so many factors promising vehicle decay, I looked at my big old rust-free 1991 GMC Suburban tow vehicle and realized I would need a city beater.

Now, most car enthusiasts who live in the rustbelt are familiar with the concept of a winter beater. This is a car that you use day-to-day when the roads are too nasty to endanger the health and well-being of your more cherished vehicles. Like a pair of galoshes, the winter beater should be warm and comfortable inside with little or no worry for its outward appearance. Most of the winter it will be covered with salt and road grime anyway, so shiny paint gets you very little extra credit. Front wheel drive is a bonus—it will drag you around in the worst of conditions— but rear wheel drive is more entertaining; you can practice your best sideways rally moves while coming home from the grocery store. Four-wheel drive, as in an old

Subaru or Audi, almost qualifies as an unfair advantage.

Moving to the city, as I had, I reasoned that whatever I found for a winter car should also be able to withstand the bump and grind of urban living during the other three seasons. I needed a car that would laugh in the face of adversity and shrug off the inevitable dents and dings. I was willing to forgo some element of practicality. Why buy a Chevrolet or Toyota when you can drive a car that is European and exciting? I wanted something reasonably reliable and roomy enough to haul wheels and tires to the tire store but more fun to drive than a school bus. Any beater should have enough standard and optional equipment to be comfortable on a short trip. Given this was a search for an all-season beater; it would be great if it had air conditioning for the summer months and a good AM/FM radio. Being a parsimonious sort, it would also be good if the car was cheap.

I figured the first thing I needed to do was to set my sights low, but not too low. Years of living in the land of corrosion have taught me a thing or two about terminal cancerous rust. It can decimate the structural rigidity of an automobile to a degree that is unsafe. While finding a rust-free example of anything seemed unlikely in southern Ohio, my focus was to look for cars that were still structurally sound.

The first logical choice for a year-around beater is a Volkswagen. Sturdy, reliable and easy to work on, Golfs and Jettas from the 1980s are also good fun to drive. Best of all is the GTi, in either 8-valve or 16-valve guise. Not that long ago, the venerable Beetle could also make this list, but the old air-cooled cars have finally transitioned into the realm of collector cars and drivable examples with minimal rust bring significantly more than I wanted to spend. Air-cooled Beetles, for all of their legendary status as great snow cars, have terrible heaters and few creature comforts.

I began my search by looking in the local classified ads, searching through the local *Auto Trader* and using the Internet. There were several possibilities in the $1,000 to $1,500 range that I had set for my search. Unfortunately, when I called about them, most were already sold. Apparently other people were also looking for cheap but interesting transportation. I forged ahead, scouring every week and making a few calls when things looked interesting. I even went to look at a few cars, but was immediately repulsed by what I considered excessive structural corrosion.

Some people consider a used car lot as the last place to look for a beater, since car dealers need significant profit margins to stay in business. Over the years, I have found that a used dealer can be a good place to find an unusual car at a cheap price. Dealers used to selling Toyotas and Hondas just don't know what to do with a Merkur, Peugeot or Alfa Romeo. They tend to put a high price on these misfits at first. When they don't sell, the cars move to the back of the lot where prices slowly sink into the ground. Unwashed and unloved, such cars can be a bargain to the beater-hunter, if you understand that an orphaned parts network may strand you and your car for weeks while you wait for a new water pump or distributor cap.

With Volkswagens clearly in such demand, I began to broaden my search. I have always liked the look of the early 3-Series BMW, the one that followed the legendary 2002 from the early 1970's. Although not very quick, the cars handle well and have some charisma. Volvos are also strong cars with good pedigrees. The rear-wheel drive versions from the 1980s were a bit dowdy, but with a bit of suspension tuning can be fun. Audis are second cousins to Volkswagens and are also a good choice for a beater. The Audi Coupe gives the stirring look of the rally bred Quattro in a front-wheel drive sports coupe. Saab also built large numbers of quirky but very enjoyable front wheel drive two and four-door sedans in the 1980s. It was one of the first companies to build turbocharged cars, but even the normally aspirated

13

versions were respectable. And then there is Mercedes-Benz. Most of its cars would be far too expensive for the cut-rate beater I had in mind, but sometimes an early 1980s diesel sedan would fall into the low price range. Parts prices on the Mercedes-Benz choice would probably make the cars uneconomical as beaters.

After looking at a lot more rust buckets and a few cars that were clearly on their last mechanical legs, I began to wonder if the age of the cheap car had come to an end. Then, one Saturday evening, I was trolling through the Internet when I found an ad for a 1989 Saab 900S. The car was less than half an hour away and the price was $1,200. I called the number and was told by the woman who answered that it had been her daughter's car, she had left for school and they just needed to sell it. Oh, and the price was now $1,000. My wife and I jumped into our car and headed across town to see the Saab.

The car was parked at the curb of a suburban home in a nice neighborhood. It was a two-door hatchback, dark blue with a blue velour interior and Saab original alloy wheels. The body had a few parking lot dings and a lightly creased right rear fender. The front bumper was missing its right side end-cap, but the piece was intact and sitting in the trunk. The rear hatch wouldn't latch properly, but stayed shut due to its own weight. The left rear fender was slightly dulled, indicating that corner had probably been repainted after a crunch. I crawled underneath the car and noticed no major puddles of oil or coolant. More importantly, the bottom of the car was free from corrosion. The owner confirmed that she had brought the car from Virginia just a year earlier.

The car had new tires on the front and almost-new ones at the rear, although of different brands. Under the hood everything looked tidy and neat and the engine oil was clean and fresh with none of the telltale murkiness that would indicate water problems from a cracked head. The pulley for the air conditioning was missing, along with its belt, but the owner had them in the trunk.

Inside, the car suffered from the usual scuffs and scrapes and the driver's seat had a few small cigarette burns and a worn patch along the back nearest the door. The other front seat was in better shape and the rear seats were unblemished. The power windows and door locks worked perfectly, as did the Pioneer in-dash stereo. The headliner was sagging badly (a chronic problem in early Saabs) but had been tacked against the backing. The car had a manual steel sunroof that worked fine. The odometer read 147,000 miles and it was time for a test drive.

The car started easily and soon settled down to a pleasing idle. The Saab 900 has a very distinctive exhaust note and the sixteen valve 2.0-liter engine sounded healthy. (For an instant I was wistful for a Saab 900 Turbo, but the added upkeep of those early-pressurized cars would all but remove them from the beater category.) There was a bit of whining from the throw-out bearing, but the car drove well. Occasionally, it jumped out of third gear when lifting off the throttle, but everything else seemed fine. All of the gauges and lights worked, except the right headlight. I couldn't see anything that I couldn't fix or that would need fixing in a beater, so I wrote a personal check and brought the car home with me for $1,000. At that price, how could I go wrong?

The next day I drove my new possession to my workshop to see what I had. The first thing to do with a new beater is to take everything out of the passenger compartment and give it a good cleaning. I vacuumed out a year's worth of dog's fur and spare change. This was also a good time to reattach the driver side door panel and give the glass a good cleaning. Next, I checked things under the hood. A trip to the auto parts store took care of the burned out headlight bulb for about six dollars. The transmission oil was topped-off and I checked brake fluid, coolant and power steering fluid levels. Next, I checked tire pressures and found both rears were very low.

When buying a beater, the condition of the tires can be very important. It is easy to spend $400 or more on new tires and that expense can be forty percent of the cost of the whole car. The stack of receipts that came with the car indicated a new set of tires had been purchased just a year earlier, and with a mismatched set on the car now, it seemed clear that rapid wear was a problem. This necessitated a trip to the alignment shop to keep the tires from wearing too quickly.

I am a big believer in checking things by-the-book and in this case the book was a shop manual for the Saab 900. I found one on eBay for nine dollars, plus three dollars shipping.

Next, I attended to the loose front bumper cover and end cap. All it needed was a re-adjustment of one of its clips that held the outer piece in place. This was easily accomplished, as was a subtle realignment of the rear latch with a screwdriver and hammer to keep the hatch securely fastened.

The air conditioner pulley was fractured at its center and I priced a new one from the Saab dealer at $80. The air conditioner helps keep the windows defogged, even in the wintertime, so it needed repair.

One thing that needed immediate replacement was the seatbelt system. I am a religious user of seatbelts, but the malfunctioning system in this Saab almost made me discontinue using them. 1989 was the year of the "motorized mouse" which car manufacturers installed to meet the requirements of automatic restraints. In my Saab, the motors that drive the mouse that carries the shoulder belts had died, making it necessary for the driver and front seat passenger to climb through a cat's cradle of webbing in order to get into the front seats. What's more, the shoulder belt flops around loosely with no chance of working as a restraint in the event of an accident. I found the solution to my problem on eBay in the form of a conventional seat belt set from a slightly later Saab 900 that had airbags and didn't need the motorized mouse system. They cost me $70, but ending the contortions required to enter the car was well worth it.

The seats and the headliner posed a longer-term problem. I hate cars with ripped seats and contemplated getting at least one of the panels on my driver seat recovered. Finding a used pair of unmarked Saab seats was another possibility. The sagging headliner problem is caused by a difference in climate between Sweden where Saabs are built and the hot climates in North America where they are sold. The foam material between the headliner cloth and its rigid board deteriorates with heat and age and the headliner slowly sags and falls. The solution is to remove the headliner from the car and either replace it (more than $400) or recover it (around $200). The third option is to recover it yourself for around $60 in materials.

So there you have it. For a total investment of less than $1500, including state sales tax and licensing, I had a reasonably stylish, fun to drive and comfortable beater. What's more, as the original body style of the 900 evolved directly from the Saab 99 of 1968, it is safe to say the car had a certain timeless appeal that still has a presence even after more than thirty years. Best of all, as the Saab 900 was a high quality car in its youth it still retained most of the crisp feel and surefootedness even with almost 150,000 miles on the clock. Sure it had more than a few dings and it would never win any car shows, but that's not why I had bought it. Most days its biggest job was carrying me from my downtown home to my inner city workshop, a distance of about three miles. More importantly, using the Saab, I could save my Suburban for gas-guzzling trailer towing, the reason for which I bought it. What's more, I would not be afraid to park my Saab on the street and even leave the doors unlocked when I left it in a parking lot while shopping. It was a city car. It was a beater. It was a title it wore proudly.

17

CHAPTER 4

But How Does it Work?
The wonderful world of technology

I was riding in a brand new domestic sport utility vehicle with the manufacturer's chief engineer. It was a press trip of epic proportions as the manufacturer wanted to have as much exposure and stories about its latest incarnation of a well-established nameplate. The engineer was pointing out the many innovative features in the vehicle, including a system that sensed rain and automatically set the windshield wipers in motion. "Interesting," I said, "How does it work?"

The engineer looked at me strangely and said, "When rain hits the windshield it is detected by a sensor and that turns on the windshield wipers." I nodded back at him and said, "Yes, but how does it work?" The man took on the look of a person speaking to someone from a foreign country. Slowly and carefully and even a bit more loudly he said, "When the rain hits the windshield it is detected by a sensor and that turns on the windshield wipers."

It was very clear now that the chief engineer thought I was pretty dense.

"No, no," I said. "You've told be what it does, I want to know how it works," I exclaimed. "Oh," he said, "You mean how the sensor detects the rain? I haven't a clue, it's some sort of magic."

I typed this column on a personal computer. Most people would tell you they know how a computer works. It's easy. You turn on the switch and wait until the computer warms up and does its internal

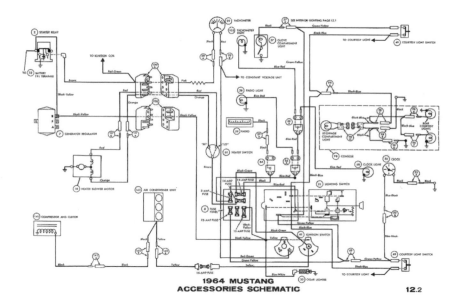

**1964 MUSTANG
ACCESSORIES SCHEMATIC**

12.2

checks. Then, after a short while, you use the mouse to point to the program you wish to use and you are on your way. But that isn't how a computer works and really isn't even what a computer does. At best it may be how you use a computer. If we really had to, some of us could vaguely recall something about binary logic and ones and zeros, but the relationship between that dimly abstract concept and typing a report or sending an e-mail or downloading a file is almost non-existent.

Each time I hit a key or move a mouse I am sending a stream of electrical energy through wires to my computer's CPU, where all of these little pieces of information get decoded, stored and recorded in the most amazing ways. There are literally hundreds of millions of them floating around at any one instant and all of them must be kept track of and held in the right place if my computer is to operate properly. When I go on-line to send an e-mail to my friend in Scotland or download the latest information about a classic car rally in Turkey, trillions of little pieces of energy must be sent and received all over the globe. I can grasp the concept, but the mind boggles at the scope and the scale of how all of this information can be kept in the proper place at the proper time. Saying you know how a computer works is a bit like saying you own an iceberg because you have an ice cube in your drink.

People used to know how cars worked. Not all people of course. Some people, even in the early days of motoring, were content to put gas into their cars and drive them until they stopped, at which point someone else could fix them. In the earliest days, cars stopped a lot. But they were simple. Anyone who had worked on a farm or factory could see and understand the workings.

Recently, I rebuilt the engine on my 1930 Sprint car. This engine is pure Model A Ford and about as simple as an automobile engine can be. It has splash lubrication and babbit bearings; technologies that many European cars of the pre-war period share. With the engine apart and in front of me, it was very easy to see how each part fit to the next and how the whole engine would work when it was assembled. I know how that engine works and what each part does. If I didn't understand some part of it, like the ignition system or the carburetor, I could undoubtedly find an old book or elderly mechanic who could explain it to me. What's more, my understanding of this simple device meant if anything were to break, I would probably be able to diagnose the problem before I took the engine apart.

Because I understand how my simple Model A engine works, I can understand how I can make it better. It is often said "form follows function." This is not strictly true. Devices generally look the way they do and improve only because what comes before them has failed in some way. In fact, "form follows failure" would be a more apt description of how things are improved. Hence the splash lubrication in my Model A Ford engine gave way to pressurized lubrication in the Ford Model B in the mid-1930s, after the Model A experienced failures when run for long distances at high speeds. The end user of such simple machines could see the problem and could describe it in a way that the engineers could use to find a solution.

The age in which we live has changed all of that. We have truly wondrous technology at our fingertips. Computers, satellites, and even our automobiles are amazingly complex and capable, but only an incredibly small number of people understand how any of it really works. Even most auto mechanics, the people who we trust to understand and correct our vehicle's faults, can tell you more about what a part or component does than how it works. This isn't a criticism of auto mechanics or our educational system. Remember, it was the chief engineer of the new sport utility vehicle who told me the rain sensor used "magic." The technology has become too complex and the concepts too abstract to be understood by anyone except the most closely involved specialist. And each specialist is so involved in their own corner of the world almost nobody is in a position to see the whole picture. As a result, because so few people understand how things work, it is no longer the end user that is the driving force for change or improvement. We accept changes and upgrades in our devices and machines, not knowing if they are really improvements or what failures or problems the technologist was trying to correct.

This brings us back to automobiles. There are two general areas where technology has dramatically changed the automotive industry. The first is the way cars are designed, tested and manufactured and the second is in the operation and control of the vehicles themselves.

Building cars has become a profoundly complex endeavor. The computer models used to predict structural stiffness, crash behavior, airflow, combustion control, fatigue life and handling behavior are among the most sophisticated ever created. Super-computers of unimaginable power are kept busy night and day spitting out results of successive iterations and refinements of the original design. The flow of information is so overwhelming that all of it cannot be digested by mere human beings. Instead, the results are synthesized into three-dimensional animated pictures that show engineers and their managers the predicted results in the form of a movie. It is only after the movie has been refined through successive passes through the super-computer that actual metal is cut and welded to build a prototype. Car companies brag about their technology removing much of the guesswork involved in developing a new car. They are so sure about their computer models that many times simulations are used in place of actual testing in order to speed the development process.

On the surface, this dependence on computer models is a good thing. The picture of a studious engineer hard at work at the computer screen designing tomorrow's cars is an appealing one. But where did the information to make these computer programs come from? And how many engineers really understand how the programs work? *When rain hits the windshield it is detected by a sensor and that turns on the windshield wipers.* Computer models are very good at working within the parameters that make up the data that went into their creation. Engineers call these limits the "boundary conditions." Working inside those boundary conditions is usually safe and predictable. That's where legal departments and social scientists would want the engineers to stay. But the interesting stuff, the stuff on the forefront of both failure and also improvement, is on the edges of those boundary conditions, outside of the abilities of the computer models. It is dangerous to allow computers to work outside of the box created by the model limits. Computers happily spit out answers without any judgment to their validity. Human intuition used to be one of the best tools to explore those boundaries, but intuition is dulled when there isn't a deep understanding of how things work. The computer projections, especially those that are presented in pretty three-dimensional movies, are accepted without the intuitive understanding of how they got there.

Nobody can deny that technology has dramatically improved the usability of the automobile. Fuel injection has replaced carburetion and direct ignition has replaced the distributor. Engine management computers control combustion to reduce fuel consumption and improve exhaust emissions, while making our vehicles fun to drive. Electronic multiplexing reduces the weight of electrical systems while anti-lock brakes, traction control, dynamic stability systems and air bags all work to help prevent a collision, or improve survivability when a collision becomes inevitable. Soon brake-by-wire and even steering-by-wire will be available. All of these systems and innovations use automotive electronics and computer control to help drivers do their job better.

But at what point do the "improvements" in our automobiles become more than we ask for or need? Do we really need to have an automatic climate control that reads the occupants' body surface temperatures and then adjusts the heating system to maintain the right temperature for each front seat passenger? Is it that much work to flip the rear-view mirror to its night setting to cut down on glare? Is it a necessity that trunks close automatically or minivan doors slide open and shut under their own power? Maybe the question isn't how the rain sensing windshield wipers work but rather why we really need them at all. Adding complexity to a system isn't always a good thing, especially if the people who must maintain it don't have a deep and intuitive understanding how it works.

I am not advocating a return to the days of ignition points and carburetor jets. Those of us who enjoy those anachronisms have our vintage cars to play with. But I am suggesting it is our duty to question everything. If you are reading this, you are an automotive enthusiast and a soldier in the battle for rationality. It is up to you and me to make sure that car companies do the right thing and use technology in appropriate ways. We can't count on the general public, they understand nothing about cars. Demand only the best from carmakers. Require them to understand what they are doing and how things work. Embrace technology, certainly, but only that technology that results in real improvement. Don't be seduced, as are so many engineers, by the glitzy world of "what can be done." Rather look at "what should be done." If something is stupid, speak up. You are the car enthusiast, you are the expert. People will listen to you. Who knows? Maybe someday when a writer asks a chief engineer how something works, the explanation will be more than just "magic."

CHAPTER 5

The Junkyard:
Social commentary and coming of age

I took my teenage son to a junkyard. Jeremy has all the indications of becoming a first class car guy. For the past couple years he has been racing a two-stroke kart and has a pair of serious radio control cars. There is talk about selling the kart to finance an MG to build into an autocross car. So a trip to the junkyard seemed like a vital step in his overall automotive education.

Not that we were going to sightsee. I needed to find a pair of usable late-model front seats to put into a vintage rally car project. The seats in the rally car were the originals, and in good shape, but didn't look like they would be comfortable after several days in the saddle. I had in mind that we might find some seats out of a recent Volkswagen, but I was willing to trust chance in our search.

The first problem we faced was to *find* a junkyard. Today they're called "auto parts recyclers" and the industry has changed dramatically. In the old days, anybody with a few acres of land out in the country could become a junkyard. Some of the best were those that were started by accident. A couple of broken down cars were pushed behind the barn, then came an offer to buy a car or two for next to nothing. The intent was to get these derelicts running, but after they sat in a field for a few years, the chances dimmed. Next, someone would come along and offer a few dollars for some of the parts off one of the hulks. Soon other cars began to appear and before long a fence was needed to keep things from disappearing. For some reason the universal choice for junkyard fence was corrugated steel sheets nailed to wooden fence posts. These quickly rusted to earth tone and savvy junkyard junkies could spot the good places just by their surrounding rusted fences.

Three factors were already working against the junkyard, however. As villages grew into towns and towns into cities, land became scarce and hence more valuable. People who moved into the newly created suburbs didn't want to live next to the junkyard eyesore and the citizenry passed laws to get rid of them. At about the same time, the price of scrap metal rose enough so that crushing a car and selling it for scrap was more financially viable than keeping it around the lot for years, selling it off part by part.

The third factor was a bit more complex. The requirements of good fuel economy and low exhaust emissions have made automobiles technologically daunting to a do-it-yourselfer. Gone are the days when a shade tree mechanic could pull a part off a junker and bolt it onto the family car to keep it running. Repairing a car today usually means taking it to a dealer so that old parts can be replaced with new parts until the problem goes away.

The modern parts recycler is a streamlined business that sometimes won't even sell its parts to the public. Wrecked cars enter the system and are stripped of their major components which are then often rebuilt, inventoried and placed on storage racks. The remainder of the car is crushed into a cube and sent on for metal reprocessing. When a mechanic orders a part it is no longer necessary to search through a yard full of cars. The engine, transmission, axle or suspension part is pulled from the shelf, ready for delivery. No doubt this makes life easier for the automotive professionals whose job is to repair late-model vehicles. However, for those of us who are upgrad-

ing or modifying an elderly project car, this system is of little value.

The first step Jeremy and I took in our search, was to look in the Yellow Pages. The category: Automobile Parts & Supplies-Used & Rebuilt. In my city, most of the junkyards—oh sorry— auto recyclers are located on the same stretch of highway on the fringe of the city. I chose two or three likely candidates, wrote down their addresses and loaded up the toolbox. This last part is critical. Some junkyards allow customers to find and remove their own parts. To do this requires a selection of tools that you must bring yourself. It helps to have an idea what sort of bolts will be used to fasten the object of your desire to the vehicle you will remove it from. I usually make sure I have a full set of sockets, a ratchet, a huge breaker bar, a large prying screwdriver and an assortment of other screwdrivers and pliers. I always bring a big hammer. Subtlety isn't what you are looking for in this type of hunting. Keep in mind that you will be lugging your toolbox over acres of landscape covered by mounds of wrecked cars so keep the weight down or bring along a teenage son to carry everything.

Remember, you need to dress the part. If you arrive at a junkyard wearing shorts and sandals, the proprietor would be justified in denying you entrance. Junkyards are dangerous places. I always bring a pair of work gloves and wear heavy shoes and jeans. In warm seasons it is not unusual to face hornets, wasps, bees and even the occasional snake. Just keep your eyes open and never put your hand into a confined space without first probing it with your prying bar or screwdriver.

So with suitable attire and fully-equipped toolbox, Jeremy and I headed out to find some seats. We cruised the junkyard strip looking for a likely candidate. The first place on our list was clearly a modern auto parts recycler. It had a chain-link fence and we could see row after row of racks holding major mechanical parts.

The next place we came to had possibilities. The large dirt parking lot was filled with pickup trucks and vans and there was a steady flow of traffic in and out. Through the open gates we could see row after row of wrecked and debilitated cars and trucks. Best of all, it had a rusting corrugated steel fence surrounding it. We parked our truck with the others, grabbed the toolbox and presented ourselves at the office near the entrance.

I told one of the old guys in the office what we were looking for. It is important to be fairly precise, I told them we were looking for a pair of seats and that the type from a Volkswagen Golf would probably work. The man pointed me in the right direction and said that we would have to remove them ourselves. Jeremy and I stepped through the back office door and out into the yard.

It was a big yard, maybe 15-20 acres, and it was filled with wrecked cars. Most of them were late model, but I was encouraged to see some models from the eighties and even a few from the seventies. Off to the left there was a section for import cars and to the right were trucks and vans. We headed straight ahead and began angling to the left toward the imports, avoiding as best we could the large puddles of muddy water leftover from the recent rainstorms.

The violence of an automobile crash is a frightening thing. Crushed body structures, torn fenders and demolished chassis were all around us. Many of the cars showed significant interior intrusion and it was sobering to think about what might have happened to a passenger who was sitting in harm's way. My son, filled with youthful excitement, was tempered by the realities of the twisted shapes which may have once carried adults to work or kids to school and soccer practice; reminders of the high price we might pay for our freedom and mobility.

In our search we encountered some foreign cars: a Volvo here, a Toyota there, a crashed Honda with its roof partially torn off by the jaws-of-life in order to rescue its occupants. There were a few Volkswagens, but I couldn't find the hoped-for GTi with its excellent and supportive seats. A Volkswagen Fox had good velour seats in gray, but we quickly found a very nice 3-series BMW from the mid-eighties with a pair of blue leatherette front seats that were unmarked. Better still, the mounting system for the tracks and adjusters would easily adapt to our project. I opened the toolbox and we began removing the seats from the BMW. We were lucky that the car was mostly rust-free so the bolts came out easily. We were careful to save every bolt and nut as we took the car apart. There is nothing worse than arriving home only to discover that in your haste you forgot a vital piece or bolt in the junkyard.

A quarter of an hour later we had the seats out and carried them across the yard to the exit. I paid for the seats and we loaded them into the back of our truck.

The two BMW seats in better-than-average shape cost me a total of $35. If I had purchased rally seats for my car they would have cost around $150 each, so the saving was tremendous. But junkyards like the one we visited are quickly vanishing. Now, a whole industry has grown up to serve the old car enthusiast with newly made reproduction parts. No need to prowl through the yards, just pick up a phone and order by mail. Anyway, most of the cars in today's yards are from the eighties and nineties. Those from the fifties and sixties are long gone and most from the seventies are best forgotten. Soon the leftover cars from the eighties will go to the crusher and only the companies that recycle modern cars will be left.

When my son has grown, and should he follow me into this life filled with old and decrepit cars, will junkyards still exist? I doubt it. Like the drive-in movie and the diner, the economic and societal forces against them are just too strong. Maybe they have outlived their need. But at least my son had a chance to see one. If you love cars, maybe you should, too.

CHAPTER 6

The Saturday Morning Environmentalist:
Trying to do the right thing

I care about the environment. I am not a tree-hugger and I am not
ready to convert my race-car to bio-mass fuel, but I try to do the right
thing when disposing of used motor oil or when choosing between
paper and plastic at the grocery store. So on a Saturday morning my
wife and I decided it was time to take the large pile of cardboard
boxes, leftover from our recent move, to the local recycling center.
The stack was so big that putting it on the curbside seemed excessive
and as it wouldn't fit into any of our cars or my compact SUV it was
clear we would need to use the truck.

Everyone should have a truck. A big truck. I know that this is a
concept that makes real environmentalists shudder, but there is nothing like a full-sized American pickup truck when you need to move
something big or a lot of somethings that are small. My truck, a 1999
Dodge Ram with a V-10 engine, actually gets very little use. Aside
from the odd hauling trip, the only thing I ever use it for is pulling my
racecar trailer around the country. For this purpose it is particularly
well suited, as it has enough torque to slow the rotation of the earth
if I drive it in the wrong compass heading. It will cruise all day long
at 70 mph with a substantial enclosed trailer in its wake and I have to
constantly remind myself that the trailer is even back there.

Anyway, it didn't take long to load the stack of flattened cardboard
into the bed of my big red truck and off we went to the recycling cen-

ter located behind the city fire station. The truck only had a quarter tank of gas in it, but we only had to go about three miles each way to get there and back. It seemed like plenty.

Things are never as simple as they seem. As soon as we arrived at the long line of green dumpsters I knew something was wrong. There was a dumpster for aluminum cans and one for plastic bottles. There was a dumpster for glass and another for newspapers. But where had the largest dumpster gone? The one dedicated to waste cardboard boxes? We got out and walked the row but none of the big green bins allowed cardboard, according to the labels. My red truck was filled with boxes and for some reason someone had suddenly decided that I couldn't recycle them here. My wife and I looked at each other while scratching our heads. Then she remembered another recycling center behind another fire station in the next town over. I eyed the gas gauge, contemplated the big V-10's voracious appetite for fuel, and decided we had just enough to make the trip. Climbing back aboard, we set out for the next recycling center.

Was it a conspiracy? Had all of the fire stations removed their cardboard recycling bins? Was cardboard recycling no longer in vogue? Do Saturday morning recycling yuppies no longer use boxes when they move? Why was I not informed? We sat in the parking lot of the fire station in the neighboring town and tried to come up with a plan. I figured if we burned the boxes in the back yard we would have produced less pollution than we were creating by driving my huge pickup truck all over the county. I knew of only one other recycling center, with a phalanx of dumpsters, located in the heart of the city. My wife suggested if we were heading in that direction anyway we may as well stop at the hardware store and pick up a few things for the yard and some salt for the water softener. It was only a little out of the way. The first hardware store only had half of what we needed so it was on to another hardware store, just a bit further afield. Two stops and a hundred and forty dollars worth of gloves, grass seed, water softener salts and an aeration pump timer later, we were back on the recycling trail. We had started out early, but by now the sun was climbing into the sky and the mercury was climbing into the eighties. We decided that searching for a place to dump a load of cardboard was hot and tiring work and we deserved some refreshment. It wasn't hard to find the Starbuck's coffee drive-thru. Eight dollars and twenty-three cents later my wife had an iced coffee and I had a mocha frappaccino. Two cups of coffee for eight dollars? This recycling was getting expensive.

Expensive? The gas gauge was continuing its downward plunge and was now touching the red zone. It was time to gas up the truck. If you own a V-10 Dodge Ram then you know that this should only be attempted by those with good credit ratings and high limits on their credit cards. I slid my card and began pumping and when the pump stopped, the charge was almost fifty dollars. Taking stock, I realized that thus far on this Saturday morning we had burned up at least ten dollars worth of gasoline, bought a hundred and forty dollars worth of indispensable items from the hardware store and consumed eight dollars worth of coffee. We still hadn't done any actual recycling.

It was with great trepidation that I turned the corner onto the road leading to the line of dumpsters in the park. My fears were unfounded, as there, resplendent in dull green paint, was the dumpster of my dreams; A dumpster that would accept cardboard. What's more, it was almost empty and our unwanted cardboard slid over the sides and gently floated downward until it covered the steel floor. It was indescribably beautiful.

As we were already on the far side of the city and quite near the storage building where we kept my wife's Alfa Romeo Spider, we decided to pick it up and bring it back to our new house in the country. We had departed in one big gas-guzzling truck and now we were returning in two separate vehicles. It was enough to make a dyed-in-the-wool environmentalist shudder. We had spent most of the morning driving around and drinking coffee and on first blush it seemed that all we had to show for it was some household supplies, grass seed and a pile of boxes in a recycling bin. Was this really social responsibility? I don't know for sure, but I do know that those boxes will rise again, recycled into other boxes that will be used by other people who are moving into their dream homes. That's the joy of recycling. Although it took us half the day, burned a quarter tank of gasoline and cost us two very expensive coffees, I convinced myself in my heart of hearts that it was the right thing to do. I do care about the environment after all.

There was also another, completely unexpected, payoff to the day, one that car enthusiasts will embrace and few environmentalists will understand. The Alfa is a happy little car and my wife looked quite jaunty wearing her Italian movie-star sunglasses while driving her Italian movie-star convertible. In its own way, the Alfa had also been recycled. It was given up by its original owner several years ago and adopted by my wife. She hadn't driven the car in almost a year and she was so happy to be zinging in its little twin-cam engine and leaving me in her dust on the back roads that lead to our new home. See? Recycling isn't just environmentally sound, it can also be fun.

CHAPTER 7

Driving Coast to Coast
If you haven't done it yet, you need to

In 1903 Horatio Nelson Jackson, a 31-year old physician from Vermont, became the first person to drive an automobile across the country. George A. Wyman had already become the first person to make the trip on a motorcycle earlier that year. Jackson and a mechanic named Sewell K. Crocker left San Francisco in May on a used 20-horsepower Winton that had a top speed of 30-mph. In Idaho, a stray Bulldog named Bud joined the pair and stayed with them for the remainder of the trip. Horatio Jackson's motivation for the trip was said to be a $50 wager that he could drive one of the new-fangled automobiles across the country in less than 90 days. This was at a time when the United States had less than 150 total miles of paved roads and almost no garages or filling stations. Even with numerous mechanical breakdowns and nearly impassable roads, Jackson, Crocker and Bud made it into New York on July 26th, just 64 days after leaving San Francisco. Jackson had won his $50, which he never collected, and had spent $8,000 of his own money in doing so.

More and More

The success of Horatio Jackson led to others making the perilous crossing that same year. Lester Whitman and Eugene Hammond drove a factory-sponsored 4.5-horsepower curved-dash Oldsmobile and E.T. Fetch and Marius Krarup made the trip on a factory-sponsored 12-horsepower Packard Model F. In 1904, Whitman reversed the journey, traveling from New York to San Francisco in an air-cooled Franklin automobile. By 1907, Whitman had the record down to 15 days and by the time the New York to Paris race made its way from New York through San Francisco in 1908, more than a dozen adven-

Jackson, Crocker, Bud make their way across the country in 1903

turesome drivers had completed the trip across the American continent. In 1909 the first woman, Alice Huyler Ramsey, drove across the country, followed by Blanch Stuart in 1910. In 1915 the silent screen actress and sometime racing driver Anita King became the first person, woman or man, to drive the entire way across the country solo.

Erwin G. Baker

Perhaps the most famous transcontinental traveler was Erwin G. Baker. In 1914, "Cannonball" Baker drover an Indian motorcycle across the country in 11 days, 12 hours and 10 minutes. In 1915, driving a Stutz Bearcat, he made the trip from San Diego to New York in 11 days, 7 hours and 15 minutes. In 1916, in a factory Cadillac, he dropped that record to 7 days, 11 hours and 52 minutes. Cannonball Baker's fastest official crossing was in 60 hours and 31 minutes from New York to Los Angeles in a Stutz, although he did set an unofficial record of 53-1/2 hours in a 1933 Graham. In 1927 L.B. Miller and J.E. Wieber upped the ante by driving from coast to coast and back in a Chrysler model 80, taking 167 hours and 59 minutes. Remember that these were the days before multi-lane interstate highways and fast food at every off-ramp.

Cannonball Run

Cannonball Baker died in 1960, but his memory was revived in the early 1970s by the exploits of automotive journalist Brock Yates. Looking to do something truly wacky, Yates proposed a no-holds-barred unlimited race from New York to Los Angeles. He called the event the Cannonball Baker Sea-to-Shining-Sea Memorial Trophy Dash. Although a half dozen crews promised to show up for the outlaw event, in the end only Yates' own entry, a team of drivers in a specially prepared Dodge Sportsman van, made it to the start. They set out from New York and 40 hours and 51 minutes later arrived on the edge of the Pacific Ocean in Los Angles, sure that they had set the outright record. The subsequent magazine stories by Brock Yates convinced others that there should be a repeat of the event and, ultimately, a tradition was formed. Yates even found time to become involved in a predictably clownish Hollywood movie about the event as the idea of driving across the country became more deeply ingrained into the minds of American automobile enthusiasts. The fastest time recorded during a Cannonball event was put up by racer Dan Gurney in a Ferrari Daytona V-12 coupe in 35 hours and

54 minutes from New York to Los Angeles. Shortly after this, Yates toned down the insanity and the Cannonball Baker Sea-to-Shining-Sea Memorial Trophy Dash became the more socially acceptable race-track to racetrack Cannonball event that it is today.

There is something magical about driving from one coast across the country to the other. It is something that every automotive enthusiast needs to do in order to earn their stripes. Sorry, you can't count that time when you were a kid and your family took that two week summer vacation that visited The Alamo, Four Corners, the Grand Canyon, Yellowstone Park, Mount Rushmore and the world's biggest ball of string. That was then, this is now. Although you can make the trip with perhaps one other person, ideally you should make it alone. When you drive long distances alone it gives you a chance to be completely in charge. You get to decide what music to play, how fast to drive, what route to take, where and what you will eat and the places you will sleep. If you want to drive for 12 straight hours, pig out on a whole bag of salt and vinegar potato chips, sing at the top of your voice along with Patsy Cline and spend a day taking only back roads, it's your choice.

It is a curious thing to travel by car across America. You get to see a transition in people and culture. People who live in the U.S. don't travel long distances by car very much anymore. Cheap airfares have taken most of the romance out of transcontinental travel. In the old days if you were to travel by horse across the countryside, let's say 30 to 40 miles a day, the change in the people and their culture would be so slow you would have trouble recognizing it. Today if you fly from city to major city, the abrupt differences are too great. But travel 500-600 miles per day in a car and you can see the gradual change in the land, the people and their culture as you drive from west to east. You have to travel at the right pace to see the changes. Unfortunately, American culture is rapidly becoming homogeneous so that the burger and fries you eat in Albuquerque and the place where you buy them will be all but indistinguishable from the ones in Terre Haute. Some say this predictability and uniformity of quality and service is a good thing, but when you are looking for adventure, you want some variety.

Looking for adventure

The choice of vehicles is surprisingly unimportant in a coast to coast journey. While choosing an old Austin Healey over a new Mercedes-Benz S-Class will clearly provide you with a different set of adventures, both will provide you with a trip that is out of the ordinary. If a car is comfortable and reliable, you get to cover ground quickly and can add numerous side trips if you wish. If your car is uncomfortable and trouble-prone, you get to stop frequently and interact with the people who live someplace other than big cities and metropolitan areas. Either way, it's a different experience than getting jammed into an airplane seat and looking down on the world from 35,000 feet. One thing people invariably ask is how do you keep from getting bored when you drive across country? The short answer is that you don't. Boredom is part of the deal. You have to learn to embrace it and learn to use it to your advantage. Boredom causes your imagination to work and your senses to seek out any sort of stimulation so that when you see a sign advertising a meteor crater or a scenic gorge or a silver mine you know you suddenly just have to see it. Boredom brings you inside of yourself and lets you decide whether or not you like the person you meet. Besides, if you get really bored, there is always the radio.

The devil in the dashboard

When you are traveling alone, the radio can be your best friend or your most obnoxious enemy. Almost every car radio has two bands,

FM and AM. Of the two, FM is better for listening to music while AM is the home of the bizarre and mundane. AM is where you usually find talk radio. In most parts of the country, day or night, the AM band is filled with at least eleven stations broadcasting listener call-in shows having something to do with stick and ball sports. If you have lived a particularly virtuous life you might, once in a great while, find a radio show that is talking about NASCAR racing, but mostly you will be in a purgatory of baseball, football, basketball and hockey. If you manage to fight your way through the sports programming you will find stations broadcasting programs with right-wing extremist hosts who find ways to blame the problems of today on the actions of previous administrations, and to discuss it *ad nauseum*. Then there are the self-help shows offering you free advice on your love life, how to raise your children, your financial solvency and how to treat your medical problems. There are always a few religious channels on the AM dial, but you can usually tell them right away by the sound of a southern preacher promising hellfire and brimstone. The only bright spot is that AM signals carry well, especially at night, and if you find something amusing you can listen to it for a hundred miles or more.

FM signals don't carry as far under most conditions. This means that a Beatles retrospective will only last for a half hour or so before it fades into static. You will be amazed that there are so many "oldies" rock and roll stations, all of which seem to have precisely the same collection of twenty-or-so old time hits. I like "Stairway to Heaven," "Hotel California" and "Surfing Safari" as much as anyone, but it does seem like there must have been a few more songs from that era that could be considered classics. Of course, you can always head toward the bottom of the FM dial and look for National Public Radio. No matter what your politics, listening to NPR's *Morning Edition* while whistling through the pre-dawn darkness, or *All Things Considered* as you head into the dusk, brings you a view of the world beyond what you can see through your windshield. There are very few national radio networks that can be counted on with such consistency. As one signal fades out, a quick twist of the dial allows you to find another station and you can pick up where the last one left off. Religious stations on the FM dial are a bit less obvious than the fire-breathing versions on AM. Religious networks have learned to mimic the sounds of more mainstream FM stations to the point that you might listen to a soft rock song or a newscast for several minutes before you realize that the station has an overtly religious message and agenda.

The latest trend for automotive listening is satellite radio, which, for a monthly fee, allows you to listen to one station anywhere in the country. Your favorite radio station signal is beamed directly from satellites to a special receiver in your car. In theory this seems a great idea, but on second thought it removes the variety in radio programming that adds to the adventure and romance of travel.

Now it's your turn

If all of this has fired up an urge within you to hit the open road, it should have. Americans are a restless people. It is in our character to explore and push beyond what is in our own backyard. From the "Corps of Discovery" of Lewis and Clark to the daredevil exploits of Cannonball Baker, crossing this continent has always been, and remains today, an adventure. Look in your garage or driveway and decide which of your vehicles will provide you with the most interesting journey. Just remember that an adventure isn't always fun, but it is always entertaining. Clear your schedule, book some vacation time and go for a drive. You will be following in some illustrious wheel tracks.

CHAPTER 8

Give and Take:
Braking in the social context

I sat on my front porch, idly watching the traffic go by. I live near the downtown of a large midwestern city and my two-lane street is a major thoroughfare for commuters heading in and out of the city center. Most people, not unexpectedly, were traveling at least five to ten miles per hour over the somewhat low 25-mph speed limit. But what caught my attention was the late braking for the traffic light at the end of my block. Vehicles came dangerously close to the end of the line of stopped vehicles before finally applying hard braking to come to a stop. As I watched this routine "hard braking" technique, it made me think of Martin Swig's theory about the beginning of the end of our civilization.

Martin Swig is a San Francisco car enthusiast. He is the organizer of the California Mille among other classic car events, a many-time competitor at the Mille Miglia in Italy and a vintage racer of great accomplishment. Swig has a theory that the introduction of disc brakes to automobiles at the end of the 1950s is a leading cause for the degradation of civilized behavior in our society. With old-fashioned drum brakes, drivers were more courteous to one another as their ability to retard the motion of their vehicles was much less than it is with modern vehicles. In the old days, drivers had to plan ahead and pay much closer attention to their driving because they couldn't count on their braking system to save them if they made a mistake.

One of the things I have to teach racing drivers when they start driving vintage cars is to change their braking technique. Modern racing cars, with their carbon brake pads and ultra sticky tires achieve the fastest lap times when the driver roars up to a corner, slams on the brakes as hard as possible, drives through a path around the corner as if on rails and then blasts down the next straight. Braking as hard as possible at the last instant is a skill that modern racing schools teach their students so they can achieve fast laps. But driving an old car with sometimes-marginal drum brakes requires a different approach. Braking needs to take place earlier and over a longer distance and the vintage driver needs to carefully blend their braking into the beginning of their cornering. John Buffum, the 11-time U.S. National Rally Champion used to describe the technique as "in like a lamb and out like a lion," although truthfully in Buffum's case it was more like in like a lion and out like a much bigger lion.

So what does driving cranky, old vintage racers with bad brakes have to do with driving in modern traffic? For mediocre drivers, maybe nothing at all. But since you are reading this essay I have to assume that you like cars and driving and want to be head and shoulders above the crowd. Many drivers seem to fixate on the bumper of the car in front of them, looking no further ahead than that to get information about the traffic that surrounds them. This can be as little as 20 or 30 feet, less than half a second away at 30-mph. If we now imagine the driver of the car in front of our driver is also fixated on the bumper in front and so on up the line, it is easy to see where one accident can cause a chain reaction.

Unfortunately, the correct solution to the problem won't make you very popular among most of the other drivers with whom you share the road. By looking far ahead of the car in front of you, you actually can see and react to things before they become an emergency. It means you can see a traffic light change from green to yellow and roll off the gas early, allowing your car to coast toward the traffic light, finally requiring only a gentle brake application to stop. The only problem is that the person behind you is glued to your rear bumper and getting angry because you haven't gone fast enough to get to the point where you both have to stop. Drive like this for a couple of blocks and you can bet that driver will find the first opportunity possible to roar past you so that they can be the first one to stop at the next traffic light. What's worse, the latest automotive technology seems to be siding with the rude person who just passed you.

The past twenty years have brought significant refinement of the whole braking process. Disc brakes avoid the fading and susceptibility to wet weather for which drum brakes were notorious. Anti-lock brakes made it possible for the driver to control the direction that the vehicle travels while under heavy braking and is especially useful in wet or icy conditions. Electronic brake distribution prevents individual wheels from locking and maintains proper brake bias whether the vehicle is lightly or heavily loaded. One of the latest innovations, Brake Assist, actually senses, from the speed with which the brake pedal is hit, that the driver is making a panic stop and applies the brakes at their maximum. While all of these innovations and applications of technology are helpful, they don't remove the responsibility for safe driving from the driver. But that may change, too.

Several car companies and automotive electronics suppliers are working on radar guided braking systems that automatically apply the car's brakes if the system senses a collision is imminent. Proponents of such a system point to how useful the system would be in fog or other low visibility conditions or in situations where an inattentive driver wasn't paying attention to the road in front of them. Am I the only one who sees a danger in such a system? If drivers now are using their brakes only to stop at the last minute, will drivers in such vehicles never use their brakes? Will they roar up to a line of traffic with their foot flat on the gas and then count on the radar-controlled braking system to bring them to a stop at the last possible instant?

Braking behavior is, of course, only one symptom of a greater problem that pop-psychologists and radio talk show hosts like to call road rage. If you keep putting rats into a cage, eventually, at some critical number, they become aggressive toward one another. Our roads have become so crowded that this aggressive behavior can be seen almost daily. Drivers push and shove, cutting each other off and working to gain two or three car lengths so that they can arrive a few seconds earlier. Rudeness is expected and drivers do all they can to meet expectations.

I spend a fair amount of the summer driving my truck and trailer to vintage racing meets all over the country. When you are towing a large enclosed trailer, you must often count on the kindness of strangers when you are merging onto a freeway or passing a long line of slow moving trucks. There was a time when drivers were willing to accept a certain give and take so that traffic could flow smoothly. Now, most drivers are long on take and short on give. Few drivers think about what happens behind them when they pull out in front of a 10,000-pound truck and trailer combination and then brake hard for the line of stopped traffic or for an upcoming off-ramp.

Sometimes you can't even win when you are trying to do the right thing. While towing my trailer home from the Pittsburgh Grand Prix, I noticed a car merging onto the interstate. I checked my mirrors, signaled my intention and moved to the left lane to allow the merging car a clean shot at the right lane. After passing the car I noticed some fast moving traffic approaching in the left lane and checking my mirror saw that the merged car was sufficiently behind me, so I could move back to the right lane. I signaled and did so. Seconds later the driver of the car that had merged went roaring past me in the left lane as his companion made obscene gestures with her hand

and mouthed obscenities to me. This bothered me. I had made room for them on the highway by moving my rig out of their way, and then when I wanted to move back into my original lane to resume my journey they were irritated at me because I was slowing them down. All take, no give.

Even leisurely drives can be graphic demonstrations of the end of courteous behavior on the highway. Most people who own old cars like to take them out and exercise them from time to time. By their nature, old cars are often slower and less maneuverable than modern machines. There was a time that people would smile and children would wave as you motored along in your ancient machine. But in growing numbers, the person who passes you is more likely to make an obscene gesture for taking up a spot on the road and getting in the way of their busy schedule. One such encounter during a drive can spoil the rest of your day.

Maybe Martin Swig is right. Maybe that bit of innovative technology known as the disc brake was the beginning of the end. Technology has a way of doing that. One of the most terrifying bits of wartime technology was the horse's stirrup, developed sometime during the eleventh century. Suddenly mounted soldiers could fight from their horse, swinging a sword with their hands and controlling their horse at the same time with the stirrup. It was a devastating weapon. It seemed so simple, it was progress and promised to make riding better and safer, yet it remained one of the most crucial weapons of warfare until the beginning of the twentieth century. By making our cars better and safer, maybe we are inadvertently making mankind less so.

CHAPTER 9

Cheap Dates:
Three ways to go vintage racing without robbing a bank.

Part One: An MG Midget For $5,000

Let's say you want to go racing. Sports car racing. Like they did in the golden age of racing with MGs, Triumphs, Jaguars, Porsches, Morgans. Skinny tires and flashing wire wheels. Let's also assume you don't have a seven figure income or a trust fund you can tap into, but you still want to experience the thrills of being on the track and racing against others. Impossible you say? I decided to find out. I spent my own money and built three project cars largely with my own hands, just like you would. I will tell you what I have learned about racing old sports cars on a tight budget. Can it be done? Perhaps, but a lot will depend first on the type of person you are.

Racing as a Personality Test

Remember the personality tests you took in high school, the ones that told you how well you handled stress and competition? If your scores indicated you were the ultra-competitive sort who should be the dictator of a small Latin American country, the idea of racing on a budget won't be right for you. Competitive? Sure. A burning desire to win at any cost? Try the Indy Racing League. A.J. Foyt might sell you a ride.

Let's Have Some Fun!

My approach is to go racing in a low-key, friendly atmosphere; to have fun driving real sports cars on real road circuits, and to do so without breaking the household budget. Some would argue that kart racing will give you the maximum racing exposure per dollar spent. No question. But go-karts, no matter how fast and intense they are, are just not real sports cars. That, and it is awfully hard to drive to the grocery store in your kart; something that is possible if you build your vintage racer the right way.

Vintage racing has grown up during the past twenty years into a nationwide pastime. From a few early events with lots of pre-war and post-war classics, vintage racing events are now popular in every part of the country. This new-found popularity has centered mostly on newer sports cars built since 1960. In fact, it is getting harder and harder to see a competing MG TC, the car that started it all in the early days of American sports car racing. Grids are nearly filled with Minis, Sprites and Midgets, Triumphs and a host of Porsche 356 coupes and roadsters. Sad in some ways, but a golden opportunity if you want to build a relatively low cost racer and join the fun.

Racing isn't Cheap

First of all, no racing is cheap, but vintage racing has two big things going for it: First, the cars that are best suited to this kind of competition were made in Europe and imported by the hundred thousands during the sixties and early seventies. British sports cars are easy to find in almost any newspaper classifieds and almost everything the Brits built in the sixties can be made into a vintage racing car. Germany, too, provides a range of cars, from early BMWs and Opels to the VW Beetle. Even Italy can contribute to the game with a range of Fiats and Alfa Romeos. True, not all of these cars will be inexpensive to prepare, but each has its loyal band of followers. An American muscle car with a V-8 engine might seem attractive from a nostalgia view, it will be very expensive to prepare and race. Better to stick with small-displacement four-cylinder sports cars and rely on nimble handling rather than brute power. That old sports car you have in your garage might be quite suitable. Most rules require a car that was built in 1973 or earlier.

The second advantage of vintage racing is more difficult to realize. It requires restraint. Examples of almost every car you will consider were and still are raced in the Sports Car Club of America. For many cars this means more than thirty years of continuous development. Unfortunately, it is very easy to build a vintage racing car to very modern specifications, one that has almost no resemblance to the car as it was raced in its original time period. Racers in the sixties were often street legal and drivable and if you resist the urge to build a modern race car inside of an old shell, your car can still be street driven, too. This has several advantages. First, it gives you a fun and attention getting sports car to drive on nice days when you aren't racing. Second, being able to drive your car on the street means you can check out systems like brakes and electrics before you get to the high-pressure environment of the track on a race weekend. The down side is that you won't be as fast as many of your fellow racers who are pushing the envelope of vintage car preparation. Frustrating perhaps, but remember my opening comments about personality types.

How Do I Get Started?

There are many vintage racing organizations in the US and Canada, each with a different set of driver and vehicle eligibility rules. The first thing to do is to contact an organization near you and get their schedule. Find out if they hold driver's school and what types of cars they allow. Go to a race and see what their club is all about. Ask lots of questions. Drivers of vintage racing cars love to talk about their cars and experiences. Maybe you fancy a Formula Vee, talk to the racers. How about that Triumph Spitfire? Be polite and ask what the strengths and weaknesses are. Get to the track early enough to watch the cars go through tech inspection. See what the inspectors focus on and look at the differences in how cars are prepared. Don't be dismayed by the mega-buck teams with their live-in transporters. Remember, they didn't exist in the sixties even for the top factory teams. At a vintage race in Silverstone in England, I saw D-type Jaguars and Lotus sports racers arriving on open, single axle trailers being towed by beat-up Ford vans. How you get there is less important than the fact you are there.

Once you have absorbed all of the information that you can, sit down and evaluate whether or not you will be satisfied running at the middle or even the back of the grid. It can be lots of fun knowing you are running a car that is much more authentic than most of the others, but it can also be discouraging if you feel like you need to keep up with the big-dollar rig across the paddock.

Choosing a Car

Three years ago, I bought a 1968 MG Midget for $2200 through the local classifieds. It had a very solid body, a reasonably intact interior and was mechanically sound. This little red car became the basis for my budget vintage racer, following the basic philosophy of keeping it period authentic and streetable. The Midget (and its cousin the Austin Healey Sprite) makes a very good first race car. It is simple as dirt, reasonably lightweight, and lots of fun to drive. In fact, Spridgets are so easy to drive quickly that they frequently give fits to bigger, supposedly faster, cars. I could have chosen a Triumph Spitfire as an alternative, but I have always had a soft spot for MGs, so a Midget was my choice.

The process of turning my Midget into a racer was surprisingly easy. I live in the Midwest and wanted to race with the Vintage Sports Car Drivers Association. I called and got a copy of their rules and set about building a racer. My first stop was Victoria British, a MG mail-order parts house. Their catalog is chock-full of goodies that I wanted for my MG, including competition front springs, lowering blocks for the rear, braided stainless steel brake lines and competition front brake pads. I splurged, too, spending $500 for a set of aluminum alloy eight spoke wheels, replicas of the Minilight wheels from the sixties. Expensive? Yes, but they make me feel so good about the car. A call to BF Goodrich resulted in a set of P175/70 R13 Comp TA R1 treaded racing tires, better by far than anything available in the sixties. While all these parts were coming, I sent the car to a local drag-racer to build a roll-over bar with diagonal cross-brace, per the suggestions from the VSCDA regulations. The roll bar was fabricated from seamless mild steel tubing and was designed to allow the use of a fiberglass hardtop like those used by the factory in international competition in the sixties.

The interior of the car was quite serviceable and didn't require any additional work. If the seat had been in poor shape, I would have found a competition seat from a racing go-kart to replace it, as space is at a premium in a Midget. I left the passenger seat in to maintain the streetable nature of the car, and also to give rides during down-time at the track. I found the bushings and wheel bearings were acceptable as they were (if I did it again, I would replace them with up-rated ones available from Victoria British) and upgraded the brakes by installing a new master cylinder. Safety is the most important criteria when building any racer, and anything suspect must be rebuilt or replaced. Starting with a solid, rust-free car will save hours of welding and bodywork that would be required to make a dodgy car sound. Almost every vintage racing club now requires a fuel cell in place of the standard gasoline tank, so I installed an eight-gallon cell mounted through the trunk floor. A hand-held fire extinguisher (with metal nozzle and bracket) attached with large hose clamps to the roll bar, competition seatbelts and shoulder harnesses and an electrical cutoff switch completed the necessary safety gear.

Almost all of the preparation work was carried out in my two and a half car garage, using regular hand tools and a fair amount of aspirin. The costs broke out like this:

Car Purchase $2200
Safety equipment: $1081
Brakes: $261
Suspension: $187
Electrical: $92
Wheels and tires: $934
Miscellaneous: $250

The total for the project was $5,005 to build a car that will pass tech inspection and be raceable with almost any vintage racing organization in the US or Canada.

There are other costs, of course. You need a flameproof driver suit, gloves, socks and shoes. An up-to-date helmet is also a requirement, and arm restraints as part of your personal gear. Most vintage racing organizations require a comprehensive medical exam and most offer a driver's school. Entry fee at the average vintage race is fairly steep at around $200 per weekend, so budget carefully. If you are lucky enough to live near a track, you could drive your car to events, but usually you will need a small trailer to transport your car. Figure about $1000 for a used trailer and hitch setup. Like I said, racing isn't cheap, but if you enjoy your experience you can spread the cost of each items over several years of usage.

Proof Positive

And so I went racing with my cut-rate Midget. Did I win any races? No, but remember, that wasn't the object. I took the car to Waterford Hills near Detroit and raced against a Mini Cooper. I took it to Grattan, near Grand Rapids, and raced with an Alfa and a Jaguar XK120. I took the car to the MG Vintage Racers feature event and ran with MGAs and MGBs and a few very fast MG TCs. In between races I took my Midget on sports car tours and a Ferrari color tour. The Midget made more than a few evening trips for ice cream and even hauled groceries. In short, I enjoyed this little car in ways that motoring enthusiasts from the sixties would easily recognize.

In all of its racing, the Midget has required surprisingly little. I broke a wheel bearing while showing my heels to a Ferrari at Waterford Hills. I did a quick head gasket change in Mosport and replaced the clutch before taking the car to Waterford for the Meadowbrook historic races in August. Other than that, routine maintenance has kept the car happy and healthy, another reason to stay with an understressed, near-stock engine. The next big item on the maintenance agenda will be rebuilding the kingpins in the front suspension, a labor-intensive but not very expensive task.

The Next Step

While my Midget represented the most popular of all entry-level steps into the vintage racing experience, I wanted to experience an even earlier type of racing. Initially, I thought of a pre-war racer. These cars are much more difficult to drive than a modern racer, lacking such seeming essentials as effective brakes and sticky tires. The costs of pre-war cars also tend toward the astronomical end of the spectrum. But there is an economical solution. Most clubs, VSCDA included, lump T-series MGs in with pre-war cars. The MG TC, TD and TF were built between 1947 and 1955 and many were imported into America. Powered by an 1250cc four-cylinder engine they are not fast, but they were the original building blocks of sports car racing in the US after the war. Brimming with nostalgia, longing for an upright radiator and separate headlights, I vowed that I would join the ranks of the pre-war drivers with my own MG TD.

CHAPTER 10

Cheap Dates 1952 MG TD
The true meaning of vintage racing

One of the really great things about vintage racing is the variety of cars that end up finding their way to the track. While a majority of the cars you'll see on a vintage weekend will be from the sixties and even the seventies, there are still enough fifties cars around to keep things interesting. Some clubs support early cars better than others. The Vintage Sports Car Club of America (VSCCA), for example, attracts large fields of pre-war and early post-war cars several times a year. The Vintage Sports Car Drivers Association (VSCDA) is likewise a haven for old cars in the Midwest. In fact, Group One in the VSCDA is reserved for "pre-war and British vertical radiator cars." Mostly, that means a few 1930s MGs and Morgans and a gangly group of early post-war MG TCs, TDs and TFs. After a season running my 1968 MG Midget with the VSCDA folks, I decided to try my hand at racing an even older car, a 1952 MG TD.

The choice of a TD was a fairly easy one. Like my 1968 Midget, this project is about vintage racing on a tight budget. That immediately removed any pre-war car from my considerations. Pre-war MGs tend to trade for amounts easily reaching $20,000, or more. While these cars are charming in their own right, they are also very expensive to keep running. The next possibility was an MG TC. These quintessential British sports cars were built right after the war, from 1947 through 1949. The prices of these cars are also quite high, nice cars

easily bringing money on the far side of $15,000 - which brings us to the MG TD. Built from 1950 through 1953, it used the same 1250cc engine and retained much of the devil-may-care look of the TC. In many ways, however, it is a much more modern sports car with better twin-leading shoe front drum brakes and independent front suspension. In spite of these refinements, its windshield still folds flat and its radiator is quite decidedly vertical. Best of all, reasonable MG TDs can still be found for under $10,000 if you are willing to wait for them. The last T-series, the TF, is appealing because of its availability with a larger 1500cc engine, but the price of these cars is closer to that of the TC.

So I began my quest for a clean, reasonably sound MG TD to use as my basis for an early vintage racer. More than 20,000 TDs were imported to the US in the early fifties, and there are still plenty around to choose from. I wanted a reasonably well-running car that was basically sound and rust-free. Because these early MGs were constructed by hammering steel panels over wooden framing, the condition of the body structure is very important to the overall soundness of the car. After several months of rejecting possible candidates in Hemmings

Motor News because of their high price, I began to wonder if I would ever find one.

Finally, while on vacation over Christmas in Florida, it happened. Less than seven miles from my parent's home was a 1952 MG TD, advertised in a local paper. I took one look at the little yellow car and knew my search had ended. The body was sound, if slightly scruffy, the seats and interior were reasonable and the engine held good oil pressure. The front fenders had been cut back, not into true cycle fenders like a pre-war car, but into a bobbed version that also did away with the running board. Most MG racers run with a cycle-type fender for the front wheels, so this modification wasn't very worrisome. This car would never be a candidate for a show-winning restoration, but it sure would make a sound basis for my vintage racer. On the down side, the transmission was very noisy and jumped out of gear, the right rear leaf spring was broken and the doors were sagging on very worn brass hinges. The owner and I haggled a bit and then settled on a price I'd seen posted on strictly parts cars; $6250 was a bargain for a drivable car. I drove the car to a storage building where it sat for a month, awaiting shipment back to Michigan.

While waiting for the car to arrive, I began to consider its preparation. I wanted a car that would be fun on the track, but also reliable on the street. I wanted to be able to take the car on local vintage car tours, to the grocery store and on picnics. This is a tall order for a 1250cc four cylinder, but the 54 horsepower XPAG unit in these MGs is more than up to the task. Rather than stress the 45-year-old engine any more than necessary, I decided to leave it stock, concentrating instead on suspension tweaks to make the car handle better on the track and the street. I also joined the MG Vintage Racers. This group of like-minded MG fanatics race MGs of every ilk all over the country. Many race MG T-types. They even published a book of ideas on how to keep your MG running better on the track. I got a copy of this MG racer's bible.

One decision I needed to make right away had to do with safety. Unlike more modern race cars, most race sanctioning bodies will allow pre-war cars to run without roll bars or fuel cells. I wasn't sure that is what I wanted to do. The argument is that pre-war and early post-war cars use the flexibility of the car's frame as a part of the overall suspension. Adding a roll over structure stiffens the chassis, changing and sometimes ruining the handling of the car. Cars that run without roll bars are not required to have shoulder harnesses so that the driver can duck into the passenger seat in the event of a roll over. *Right.* I decided to take my TD to my local drag race shop and have them build me a simple $250 roll over hoop that attached firmly to the car's steel frame.

The next safety question was a fuel cell. One of the most distinctive elements of an early MG is its slab gasoline tank strapped across the back of the car with its quick release flip-open filler cap: Very racy, a little vulnerable. I decided the risk of fire was not too great and that I could minimize it by keeping the tubular metal framework of the spare tire carrier on the outside of the tank and by drilling a couple of small holes into the flip-open cap, I could hold it tightly closed with safety wire. Admittedly not as safe as a fuel cell, but a fair nod to tradition and safety.

The car arrived by transport truck to snow-bound Michigan at the end of January and immediately went into the garage and up onto jack stands. Off came the wheels and I began completely disassembling the suspension. Early MGs have fenders that come off easily; since mine were scratched on the edges, I took them off and sent them to the paint shop. I ordered new parts for the front and rear suspension. The front suspension of an MG TD is nearly identical to that of an MGB, which makes it easy to upgrade for racing. I ordered front springs for an MGB GT, which are significantly stiffer than the stock MG TD springs, and a 3/4 inch front anti-roll bar and mounting kit, also a part for an MGB. I put in urethane suspension bushings and heavier oil into the lever arm shock absorbers. For the rear, I ordered new leaf springs for both sides and a set of uprated spring eye bushings. I also put heavier oil into the still-usable rear lever arm shocks.

The MG TD uses drum brakes with twin hydraulic cylinders in each front wheel and a single cylinder in each rear. I bought new cylinders for each wheel and a new master cylinder. The master cylinder on this car is a single circuit, there is no back-up. If the system fails *you have no brakes.* Some racers have adapted a dual master cylinder to their T-Series MGs, but I decided to use brand new stock components and to maintain them religiously. Remembering that the car was already 45 years old, I also replaced the steel brake lines and put new rubber brake hoses on each corner. Stock brake shoes were my choice for lining material and I put new wheel bearings on the front wheels.

The body was already reasonably presentable, with a nice patina of age that old cars seem to get if they haven't been restored. I replaced the sagging door hinges and replaced a dry-rotted timber in the driver's door. Other than that, the body was particularly sound, having led an easy life in the Florida sun. The problem with the transmission was eating away at my subconscious until, finally, I pulled up the floorboards and shipped the worn out four-speed unit to University Motors for a rebuild. It was expensive. Very expensive at nearly $800. While the transmission was out, I took advantage of the time to take care of the cockpit. The floorboards of an MG are made from wood, 3/8 inch plywood to be specific. Using the old ones as patterns, I made up a new set, from 1/2 inch plywood and bolted them firmly to the car's steel frame rails. Anchoring points for the competition seat belts were also found on the steel frame instead of the wooden floors— an obviously poor place to mount the belts. I drilled a large hole in the wooden dashboard and mounted the required electrical cutoff switch.

With the car coming together and the fenders at the paint shop I had to decide on a color. I have always liked the "cream crackers" yellow and brown paint scheme of the pre-war MG racing team and so I specified a Jaguar brown color for the fenders. When they returned from the paint shop at a cost of about $300 I wasn't so sure I had made the right choice. Even with the fenders sitting next to the car, I just wasn't sure. Fortunately, when I bolted them on, everything fell into place and the car looks distinctive and period, the kind of pre-war look I wanted. A long leather strap and brass buckle to keep the hood closed over bumps finished the 1930's look. I chose Michelin XZX radial tires, with inner tubes in size 165R15, and mounted them on the stock steel wheels. The tires are tall and narrow by modern standards, but right for this kind of car. They run about $60 a piece, plus another $10 or so for each inner tube.

You may have noticed I haven't mentioned much preparation to the engine. Aside from rebuilding the generator, replacing the canister oil filter with a spin-on adapter unit and replacing the bulky stock air cleaner with a K&N filter, not much was done. Reliability was my goal. The engine had good compression and oil pressure and I decided to see if the car would be competitive with its stock complement of 54 horsepower. I had a local muffler shop place a muffler (the resonator for a Chrysler minivan actually) and exhaust pipe on the car to make it street legal. The cost here was a very reasonable $40. I was also careful to add an additional throttle return spring to meet the vintage racing rules.

And so I put the TD on the road. Spring is a delightful time for an open sports car, even one that can only manage 0-60-mph in something around 20 seconds and has a top speed of 75-mph or so. But driving the car helped me find several little problems that I could put right before they became major concerns on the racetrack. Besides, it was just fun. Finally, the date of my first race with the TD arrived and I put the car on a trailer for the long tow to Blackhawk Farms in northern Illinois.

Upon arriving at the track, I was immediately guided into a parking spot alongside a host of other Group One cars by Tom Moore. Long-haired and bearded, Tom is a computer programmer by day and the spiritual leader of the VSCDA Group One on race weekends. His beautiful MG TC has been a fixture on Midwest tracks since vintage racing started in the seventies. Many, including Tom, had driven their cars to the track that day and would drive them home again at the end of the weekend. We were a motley group, a dozen or so cars with upright radiators and skinny tires. Mostly MGs, mostly TCs, few with roll bars. The grid for the first practice session looked like 1952 revisited.

I was very happy to find my TD was easy to drive. Although lacking real horsepower, the car was fun on the track. Going fast in a T-series involves letting the tires slide a bit on the way into a corner, getting on the power early and, most of all, not using the brakes very much. The idea is to carry as much speed through the corner as you can, as the engine won't help you with very much acceleration on the exit. Great fun, especially when you are running side by side with two or three other cars that are trying to do the same thing. If my car wasn't very fast, neither were the others.

Saturday afternoon's pursuit race was my finest hour of the weekend. In this race the slowest car starts first, followed at intervals by successively faster cars. At the end of ten laps all of the cars should approach the finish line at the same instant. My MG flew over Blackhawk's scenic course and I crossed the line in second place, literally inches from the fishtail exhaust of a 1930s MG racer.

Sunday afternoon didn't go as well. On the third lap of the feature race, while threatening third place, the TD began to run rough. Coming down the straight, it ran worse. Braking for the corner I noticed smoke rolling out from under the hood and into my face shield. I looked down and saw the entire cockpit had filled with flames. I began to smell burning wood, not a great thing in a timber frame car. The float chamber on one of the SU carburetors had come loose, dumping raw gasoline directly onto the hot exhaust manifold. This quickly caught fire and was burning merrily as I drove. I pulled to the side quickly, jumped out and set to work with my fire extinguisher. The blaze was quickly out, but not before all of the paint had blistered from the hood. Soot covered everything and the under hood was a melted mess of charred wires and fuel lines. It was a pity, but repairable. I realized that this sort of accident could have just as easily happened on the highway while driving, so I was fortunate to be wearing two layers of fireproof clothing and to have corner workers close by when it happened.

Rebuilding the car after Blackhawk Farms, I set about to ensure that the same problem would never repeat itself. First of all, I drilled holes into the bolts holding the float chambers onto the SU carbs. Then I drilled a tiny hole into the casting of each carb, and twisted a piece of safety wire into place to prevent the bolts from loosening and falling out. Next I replaced the normal rubber fuel line with braided stainless steel covered line. The old rubber-covered lines were charred into crumbling pieces by the under hood fire and I didn't want a repeat. Most auto parts stores carry these lines and the cost was around $60. I took the hood panels to the paint shop and had the top portion painted Jaguar brown to match the fenders, while the side panels were painted their original yellow. The cost was another $300. After a month of work, the car was ready to go back to the track, not much worse for its frightening experience.

The next two races were as different as they could be. Waterford

Hills is a tight twisty track outside of Detroit. It was the site of the MG Vintage Racers annual gathering and was attended by many of the fast T-types from the east coast. Too fast, it turns out. My stock TD, which was a solid upper mid-class car in VSCDA races, was way outclassed, perhaps the reason so few of my Midwest brethren chose to attend. The East Coast group runs cars that have been modified way beyond streetability, into the realm of out-and-out racers. Fun, but ultimately frustrating for me on what is my home race track.

The next race was at Elkhart Lake in the fall with my companions at VSCDA. This is an extremely long circuit, especially in an MG TD. Eighteen pre-war and vertical radiator cars showed up for the race and I had a great time, ultimately qualifying sixth and finishing fifth. At the start, I was side by side with John Kleen's Bugatti Type 35. The sound of that tiny straight eight accelerating away from me at the first corner was worth the whole price of admission. The race finally settled down and I found myself in a furious battle with the poetically named Frenchy Dampier in another MG TD. Lap after lap we would pass and re-pass, the crowd and even the corner workers were on their feet and cheering. This is what vintage racing is all about. This is what racing in VSCDA Group One is all about. In all, I had spent about $11,000 preparing my MG TD to race in this group. My car isn't competitive with the fast cars from the east; it would require a fully modified racing engine for that. But here, among friends, it gave me some of the most enjoyable racing I have ever experienced. To me, my MG TD is the whole reason for going vintage racing.

CHAPTER 11

Cheap Dates 1969 MGB GT
Faster, faster you fool

Sooner or later in your vintage-racing career, the bug will hit you: *The need for speed.* I have told you how to go vintage racing on a tight budget. The object was to have fun running in the middle of the pack with cars that don't cost a fortune. But after a while, you will want more. You'll want a faster car, quicker lap times, more glory. I set out to find all three.

I chose another MG for my glory hunter, this time an MGB. Some might correctly argue that an MGB is not really the best basis for a killer racing car, and largely, they would be right. First of all, it is fairly heavy. Secondly, it has a fairly crude suspension setup using leaf springs at the back and lever-arm shock absorbers all around. Lastly, it has a long-stroke 1800cc engine with only two intake ports to be shared among its four cylinders. On the plus side, the MGB has been raced continuously since its introduction in 1962 and a lot of know-how has been developed to make them go faster. The cars are readily available. Even the competition parts patterned after those available from the factory are not very expensive. The MGB is also the quintessential British sports car from the sixties.

Because they made so many MGBs in the period between 1962 and 1973, finding one really isn't a problem. Finding one that hasn't rusted away to dust is a bit more of a challenge, especially in the heart of the Midwest's rustbelt. I used the internet and found a racer in Connecticut who had several MGBs for sale. A deal was struck. He would do the initial suspension and brake work on a rust-free 1970 MGB and equip it with a strong stock engine that featured a 45 DCOE sidedraft Weber carburetor. This intake setup would be typical of a factory car in the sixties. He would also install a roll bar and do whatever minor body work was needed before painting the car. All this for $3000.

Two months later I received a phone call. The car he was building, my car, was at the body shop and a problem had arisen. Sometime in the car's past, it had been heavily crashed and a new nose grafted on -- not the best foundation for a racing car. He had a solution, however, in a 45,000 mile, one-previous-owner 1969 MGB GT. Now many will say that the hardtop grand touring version of an MGB isn't a good starting point for a racer. It weighs even more than a roadster (about 200 pounds more) and it has more frontal area than a roadster without a windshield. On the other hand, this particular car was completely rust-free, having been stored for almost twenty years inside a parking garage. Sight unseen, I made a decision to go head with the MGB GT.

By now it was mid-May, and the prospects of racing the car during the season were still bright. I decided to give myself plenty of time and target the Meadowbrook Historic Races at challenging Waterford Hills on the first weekend of August as my first race with the MGB. I began ordering the parts I would need to make my car a legal racer. A 12-gallon fuel cell ($350), competition seatbelts ($120 for both driver and passenger), an electrical cutoff switch ($52) and a set of BF Goodrich Comp T/A R1 competition tires ($600). Parts began arriving and I made weekly phone calls to my car builder, hoping for progress reports. Mostly I heard excuses for why my car hadn't been painted yet. Still, I was told the suspension and brakes and engine were all being worked on and the car was coming along just fine.

By mid-July I was worried. If the work wasn't being done to a high enough standard, I would have to redo much of what was being done in Connecticut before I could race. Would there be enough time? I voiced my concerns and was again reassured that all would be taken care of. With time running out, I sent the fuel cell on to Connecticut for installation. The change over from wire wheels to steel wheels was also being held up. "Oh well," I thought. I always liked the look of wire wheels and I could purchase some knock-off alloy wheels to use with my treaded BFG racing tires. The chances of having the car delivered in time for Waterford were beginning to look slim. I called a transport company and arranged ($500) to have the car picked up the day after returning from the paint shop and two weeks before the vintage race.

The car arrived on Monday. My mail-order bride wasn't exactly as I had pictured her. The body shop had done a very sloppy job with her red paint and she still wore masking tape in places. Mechanically, it was clear that the lever arm shocks were shot, the front springs were sagging and a quick look confirmed very worn suspension bushings in the front. A tentative stab at the brake pedal hit the floor and the only electrical systems working were the ignition, electric fuel pump and brake lights. *This was a car that was supposed to be ready to race as delivered?*

As bad as it was, there were still some good points. The body shell was indeed rust-free and the installation of the fuel cell, sometimes a bit tricky, was very well done. The engine started easily, had good oil pressure and idled smoothly with its Weber carb. I grabbed my Victoria British catalog and ordered a stack of parts. Next Day Air delivered a new brake master cylinder ($186), stainless steel brake lines ($77), a negative camber kit for the front suspension ($88), lowered front coil springs ($50) and competition front brake pads ($80). I also ordered competition shock valves for the lever arms, some

heavy duty shock oil and a host of smaller parts. The clock was running and I cleared my calendar and threw myself into the project.

The first time I actually drove the car was a week later. One advantage of a vintage racer that is still streetable is the ability to test out brakes, ignition timing and engine cooling before you get to the track. After five days and late nights of thrashing, the car stood ready to go. Not everything was exactly as I wanted it, but I had brakes, suspension and tires, and the engine ran well. The rest could wait until the next race.

Waterford Hills is an excellent track to find out if you have done your suspension homework. It manages to cram twelve turns into a little more than one mile, keeping the driver very busy. My first session of Friday was quite satisfying. The engine pulled well out of the slow corners and the car had plenty of grip through the faster ones. I took it easy at first, feeling out the MG to make sure all was as it should be. During the first session, I noticed the rear brakes getting very hot and I wasn't using them that hard. The second session

Friday afternoon went equally well, and I settled down to exploring the handling of my new racer.

The first thing I noticed was that I had grip. Lots of it. The BF Goodrich tires were sticking so well that I had to hold myself into the seat in tight corners. There was none of the sliding that I enjoy so much with my much more vintage 1952 MG TD. In fact, the car was much more like a present-day racer, thanks to these very modern radial tires. Is that a good thing? It is if you want to go fast. It may not be if you wish to recreate the experience of racing a car as it was in its own time. But, I rationalized: *if I run something less grippy, I won't be able to race with the faster cars.* I hadn't realized it yet, but I had already begun sliding down the same slippery slope that all of vintage racing is heading.

Saturday was a practice session, a qualifying session and a race. Practice went fine as I began to use more of the car, cornering harder and accelerating sharply away from corners. Next came qualifying. I decided to try hard and see what my racer could do. After two laps, while in the middle of a sweeping right-hander, I suddenly heard a clattering noise from the engine and noticed a drop in oil pressure. Pulling into the pits, I knew immediately that my race weekend was over. All that hard cornering had starved a rod bearing. The same thing had happened to the factory team at Sebring in 1963, and I doubt their bias-ply racing tires provided the same grip as my modern BFG radials. Sadly, with the dark despair that comes to all who have broken their racers, I put the MG onto the trailer and took it home.

I let the MG sit for a week while trying to decide a course of action. I knew that there were several things I needed to do to improve the car on the track. I ordered a racing seat ($150) to better keep me behind the wheel. I ordered some competition rear brake shoes ($131) to prevent the overheating I had experienced. Finally, I tackled the engine problem. Out came the engine and upon inspection it was clear that the number-two rod bearing had destroyed itself, due to a lack of oil. The solution was a high volume oil pump ($142) and a baffled oil pan, created for me by a local MGB racer for $325. The rest of the engine was in reasonable condition, but I couldn't resist the temptation to do some modifications for more performance.

First, my machine shop reconditioned the bottom end, resizing several connecting rods and grinding the crankshaft for new main and rod bearings. Because my goal was more performance, I decided against reusing the original pistons and purchased a set of new stock ones in .030 overbore size ($250). A new high lift, half-race cam kit ($350) with lifters and pushrods would help the Weber breathe better, as would skimming the cylinder head to get a compression ratio of about ten to one. A high-flow exhaust header ($130) finished the engine package and a competition clutch disc ($54) went in to help transmit the hopefully greater horsepower. In fact, the level of preparation of my engine is very similar to what the factory cars would run at a long distance event in the sixties, producing about 125 reliable horsepower.

Bolting everything back together and into the car was a task I left to long-time British sports car racer and mechanic Steve Steeb at his garage in Ann Arbor. This is a fairly critical juncture, as British cars tend to leak copious quantities of oil unless they are carefully assembled using modern sealants and gasket compounds. With everything back together the MG was ready to take on another racetrack, for another vintage race weekend.

And so, off I went to Gingerman Raceway, on the western side of Michigan, for a one-day vintage race with the Midwest Council of Sports Car Clubs. I had always wanted to race with this laid-back group and their one-day Sunset Sprints seemed like the perfect chance to test out my new engine. My group consisted of a collection of cars that included an Alfa Coupe, a Porsche 914, a couple of 240Zs and a very fast Volvo 142 sedan. With a brand-new engine, I decided to take it easy and used a fairly low 5,000-rpm redline in my practice and qualifying sessions. During the race, I extended that upward another 500-rpm, trying to maintain the discipline of that limit, even in the heat of racing.

The first thing I noticed with my new and improved racer was the difference a proper racing seat made. Instead of gripping the wheel tightly to keep from sliding around the stock seat, I could hold on gently and let the hip-hugging side bolsters of the custom seat do their thing. Next, the improvement in braking from the competition rear shoes meant I could go much deeper into corners and really use the brakes to slow the car down. But, of course, the biggest difference was in the engine. Even with a conservative rpm limit, the engine pulled cleanly, with authority, and the car felt quick and lively out of the corners. This was the feeling I was looking for when I started this project. A production car turned racer.

The feature race came and I was mid-grid, behind the Porsche, just ahead of one of the Z-cars. The green flag dropped and the fight was on. For three laps I was glued to the tail of that Porsche, working to find a way around him. Then, on the fourth lap, at the end of the front straight, the seal on the oil filter blew out, dumping oil all over my rear tires. A quick trip through the infield, fighting for control on the slick grass, and my race was over. Oil covered the entire engine compartment, but I was lucky enough to turn off the engine before any damage had occurred. After bringing the car home, I cleaned up the mess and fitted a new oil filter and a new pressure relief spring to reduce the amount of pressure my overachieving oil pump sent through the filter.

So, aside from this minor mechanical problem, I had achieved my goal: building a racer with a stronger-than-stock engine, but one that is still streetable and will be very reliable. I spent about $8500 on this project. Considerably more than the bargain-basement $5,000 I had spent on my MG Midget, but much less than the $11,000 my charismatic but very slow MG TD had cost.

What have I learned? First of all, there is way too much emphasis on racing in vintage racing. In theory, the battles between these cars have already been fought, the winners crowned and the losers vanquished. The object should be less a continuation of a competition career for an old war-horse than it should be a celebration, experiencing the way it was to race these cars in their own period. Using modern tires, suspensions and engines to make a modern racing car that just looks old doesn't give back the same sensations as running a car to its true period specifications. By bolting modern tires onto my MGB, I created the lubrication problem that ultimately caused me to rebuild the engine. But using those tires is absolutely necessary if you want to be competitive and makes the car handle much better than any MGB ever did in the sixties. If you bring a vintage car to a vintage race, you might as well be driving around the track by yourself. Everyone else, even the tiny low-performance cars, will be off in the distance, beneficiaries of the dramatic improvements modern technology can bring.

For me, vintage racing has never been as much about going fast as it is about having fun. In the course of building and racing three different MGs, I discovered that a cheeky MG Midget, given the right circuit, runs rings around bigger and supposedly faster cars. I discovered that the genteel pastime of vintage racing is very different than the currently popular racing of vintage cars. I also discovered that building and racing a fast car like my MGB, as enjoyable as it is in its own way, didn't give me as much enjoyment as racing my quirky, charming and desperately slow MG TD.

CHAPTER 12

An Echo of the Past
The History and Evolution of Twin-Cam Engines

In the mid-1980s, automotive engineers "discovered" multi-valve engines. A regulatory push for lower exhaust emissions and higher fuel economy, coupled with customer demand for cars that could and would perform as well as cars from a generation earlier, led car companies to design powerful and efficient four-cylinder engines. A horsepower race of sorts had developed and small displacement engines could produce big numbers if they ran at high engine speeds.

Four Are Better Than Two

To help these small engines breathe at high speed required large intake and exhaust valves. But the combustion chamber size limits the size of the valves and it was found that two small intake and two exhaust valves would breathe more efficiently than a single large intake and large exhaust valve. This was especially true in the short-stroke, high-speed engines that were popular in Europe and starting to show up in America. But the angle at which the intake and exhaust valves enter the combustion chamber also affects gas flow, and activating the valves with a single camshaft was difficult if the optimum valve angle was to be maintained. Enter the twin overhead camshaft engine.

Actually, twin-cam engines entered a lot sooner than the mid-

1980s. In fact, right from its inception in the early 1900s, the twin-cam has remained the engine to beat on racetracks from Indianapolis to LeMans.

In the Beginning

Gotlieb Daimler created the first automotive internal combustion engine in 1885. In 1891 Peugeot produced its first automobile, a Daimler-engined quadricycle, and in 1894 finished second and third in the world's first organized auto race, held between Paris and Rouen. By the early 1900s Peugeots were regular competitors, usually running small car classes with huge single-cylinder engines with great success. In 1910, Paulo Zuccarelli beat the mighty Peugeot team with a small-displacement four-cylinder Hispano-Suiza. Peugeot drivers Jules Goux and Georges Boillot knew they needed a new kind of engine and convinced Zuccarelli to join their team. They went to Robert Peugeot, the president of the company with an idea. They proposed an all-new racing engine to enter the Grand Prix circuit. He liked the idea so much that he commissioned a car from the three drivers as well as another car from young Ettore Bugatti. Peugeot decreed that the faster of the two designs would win the Peugeot name and the contract.

Les Charlatans

The three racing drivers, knowing they were in over their heads, added Ernest Henry from Switzerland to their team. Henry is a bit of an enigma. Variously described as merely a draftsman or as the true genius behind the new design, little is known about his formal engineering training. He had worked at one point for Picker, a marine engine company in Geneva, and no doubt picked up much of his practical knowledge there. One thing is certain, the engineering staff of Peugeot did not like the idea of a small team of drivers

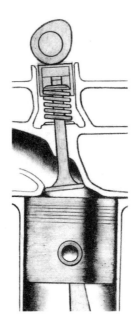

and outsiders designing their racing cars and labeled the group *Les Charlatans*.

Bugatti built a car whose best speed was 99-mph. *Les Charlatans* beat that by more than 15- mph and Robert Peugeot gave his name to their car. In fact, the complex racer carried not one existing Peugeot part. What it did have was a beautifully executed 7.6-liter twin over-head camshaft sixteen-valve four-cylinder engine with a modern hemispherical combustion chamber. But this engine wasn't the first to use two camshafts. They had been used before, located in the cyl-inder block of relatively inefficient T-head engines. In 1905 Delahaye had experimented with a double overhead camshaft with six inline valves-per-cylinder for a marine-racing engine and set a new world's speed record on water. But *Les Charlatan's* Peugeot was the first automotive application of the twin overhead cam concept and set the pattern for all future twin-cam designs. The first race the team entered was the Grand Prix de l'ACF at Dieppe on June 26, 1912. Boillot beat the favored 14-liter Fiats by 12 minutes after two full days of tough racing. The following year, Jules Goux took the twin-cam Peugeot to Indianapolis and beat the field by 13 minutes after 500 miles.

The Great War

Les Charlatans didn't last long. Zuccarelli was killed in practice shortly before a Grand Prix in 1913 and Boillot went into the French air force during the war and was killed in a dogfight with the Germans. Jules Goux also entered military service and after the war continued racing, including a few more attempts at Indianapolis in the 1920s. Ernest Henry, unhappy with his treatment by Peugeot's mainline engineers, left the company and designed twin-cam racing engines for Ballot and Sunbeam in the early 1920s. He eventually fell into obscurity and died in poverty in 1950. His Peugeot twin-cam engine, perhaps one of the most successful racing engine designs of all-time, became the model for a large number of copies from companies like Delage, Fiat and Nangent in their racing cars. It was also the starting point for Harry Miller's brilliant run of racing engines that, as Offenhausers, were still winning races in the mid-1970s.

A Good Concept

A number of other twin-cam racing engines appeared in the early to mid-twenties, mostly from English and French companies. In 1921, American Fred Duesenberg brought the twin-cam concept to his racing engines and won the Indy 500 in 1924, '25 and '27. In 1928 he established a twin-cam production engine for the company's superb line of high-performance luxury cars. Stutz followed in 1931 with the 32-valve eight-cylinder DV32. Alfa Romeo built its first twin-cam engine as far back as 1914, a one-off 4.5 liter four-cylinder Grand Prix engine, but it never ran in international races. Alfa was to become one of the twin-cam's greatest proponents through the efforts of Vittorio Jano, beginning in 1926 with the highly successful 1500cc and later 1750cc six-cylinder sports cars. In supercharged form, these cars won all the great sports car races except LeMans from 1928-30. LeMans fell to Alfa from 1931-34 with Jano's next design, a 2.3-liter straight-eight with double overhead cams. The same engine also powered Alfa's successful Grand Prix car of the period. In 1934, Jano's 6-cylinder twin-cam 2.3-liter engine became the Alfa engine of choice and remained in production into the early post-war years. Bugatti entered the twin-cam ranks in 1931 with its Type 51 straight-eight, a twin-cam development of the very successful Type 35 single overhead cam engine. The twin-cam owed most of its valve-train design to a pair of Harry Miller's racing engines that Bugatti had purchased and carefully examined in 1929.

Mercedes-Benz began experimenting with twin-cam engines in 1922 under technical director Paul Daimler. Ferdinand Porsche took over his duties when Daimler left the company at the end of 1922 and oversaw an Indianapolis effort in 1923 that resulted in 8th and 11th place finishes. Ultimately, these early efforts led to the twin-cam engines in the all-conquering Silver Arrow Mercedes Grand Prix cars of the late 1930s.

The Jaguar XK

While specialized racing engines and virtually hand-built Duesenberg and Stutz models took advantage of the better breathing afforded by double overhead camshafts, very few production cars, particularly those made in America, had anything more sophisticated than side-valve engines through the end of the thirties and into the forties.

In fact, overhead valves were considered quite advanced when they appeared on Oldsmobile's Rocket V-8 engine and Cadillac's V-8 of 1949. That's why William Lyon's remarkable double overhead cam six-cylinder Jaguar XK engine seemed so radical when it was introduced in 1948. William Heynes, Walter Hassan and Claude Baily designed this engine (which remained in production through a number of iterations well into the 1980s) during the war. The double overhead camshafts were chain driven, greatly simplifying the gear drive systems that were popular before the war. Its original purpose was to power a luxury sedan, the Jaguar Mark VII. To advertise the new engine Lyons had a sports car built around the new engine for the 1948 Earl's Court motor show, and the XK120 was born. The car was a hit, as was the MK VII sedan of 1950 that the engine was originally created for. But the XK120 was pure glamour and, in time, this engine became the definitive sports-car engine. It powered Jaguar cars to victory in the 24-hour race at LeMans no less than five times.

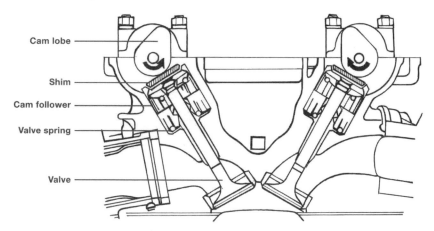

Cam lobe

Shim

Cam follower

Valve spring

Valve

Others

The clever Jaguar engine was joined by a twin-cam six-cylinder engine in 1950 in the Aston Martin DB2. Aston Martin had experimented with twin-cam engines in the early 1920s. The new engine, originally designed by W.O. Bentley for the 1948 Lagonda, had a long and useful life in Aston sports cars and led to a LeMans win in 1959.

1950 also saw the introduction of the new 1900cc four-cylinder from Alfa Romeo. This engine marked a departure for Alfa from a small maker of expensive and prestigious sports cars to a large-scale producer of mainstream automobiles. Lightweight and powerful, the 1900cc engine formed the basis of Alfa engines for the next three decades. The 1300cc twin-cam came in 1954, followed by 1600cc, 1750cc and 2000cc versions. These were high volume engines, yet were beautifully made and delightful to listen to, whether in a sedan or sports car.

Other small but highly successful Italian sports car manufacturers like Maserati and OSCA and Spanish builder Pegaso turned to twin-cam designs in the early through mid-1950s with great success. Ferrari joined the twin-cam ranks in 1949 when Aurelio Lampredi converted Gioacchino Colombo's single-cam V-12 Formula One engine, but it wouldn't be until the 1960s that a Ferrari GT car would be available to the public with a twin-cam engine.

Following his success with the Jaguar engine, in 1953 Walter Hassan joined with Harry Mundy of BRM V-16 fame to create the 2.5-liter Coventry Climax V-8. Although not immediately successful, this engine led to the highly successful 1.5-liter Coventry Climax four-cylinder engine for Formula 2. Used by Lotus and a wide range of other racing car builders in England, the Coventry Climax engine was lightweight and powerful. It was popular in both sports car and formula car racing.

Aurelio Lampredi moved to Fiat from Ferrari and in 1966 introduced the 124 Sport that used twin belt-driven overhead camshafts. The Fiat 124 with its twin-cam engine came at a time when most other inexpensive sports cars, like the MGB and Triumph TR4, were still using pushrod engines. The use of a rubber toothed belt by Fiat made the engine much quieter and less expensive to build than previous twin-cam designs. The Fiat twin-cam remained in production well into the 1980s and was used in sports cars, coupes and sedans.

Ford

Also created in the sixties were two Ford twin-cam engines, neither of which was actually designed by Ford. The Lotus twin-cam used a Cortina four-cylinder engine block, topped with a special twin-cam cylinder head. Used in Lotus sports cars and Ford sporting sedans like the Lotus Cortina and Ford Escort, the engine was a great success, especially in competition. In 1967, Keith Duckworth and his Cosworth Engineering company designed another Ford-based project, the Ford Cosworth V-8. Highly competitive, readily available and extremely reliable, the Ford Cosworth DFV Grand Prix engine and DFX Indy car engine opened the modern era of professional racing and remained viable for more than a decade.

New Problems To Solve

By the time the 1980s arrived with the seemingly conflicting needs for high efficiency, low emissions and good performance, the twin-cam concept had already been in use for nearly seventy years. Toyota, with the Corolla FX16, was one of the first Japanese cars that came to the US with the exotic valve-train. Soon many cars from Japan carried the 16-valve double overhead cam four-cylinder engines that signified performance to a whole generation of enthusiasts who had never heard of a Peugeot Grand Prix car or a Coventry Climax engine. In time, refinements appeared – like the Honda Prelude with variable intake-valve-timing to improve power and emissions, a concept that had been introduced first by Alfa Romeo earlier in the decade.

One Good Idea

American manufacturers, once among the leaders in twin-cam technology with Duesenberg, Stutz and Miller, were slow to catch up. Pushrod overhead valve engines had become so entrenched that the introduction of a special Vega with a Cosworth twin-cam cylinder head in the 1970s was considered to be exotic in the extreme. But in the beginning of the 1990s, American manufacturers developed engines that used the technology. Even the Corvette, a long holdout for pushrod engines, was available for a time with a ZR-1 V-8 engine whose complex twin-cam cylinder head came from Lotus Engineering and was manufactured by Mercury Marine. Today most European automakers are heavily invested in twin-cam multivalve engines. Ford, Daimler Chrysler and General Motors, as well as Japanese companies, have twin-cam engines in production. But look at them closely and it is easy to see that their theory, design and execution still display the original concepts Ernest Henry and *Les Charlatans* pioneered in that 1912 Peugeot.

CHAPTER 13

Saving Lives:
It isn't so hard when it's the right thing to do

There is little doubt that safety systems in modern automobiles save lives. Thanks to the efforts of researchers and engineers around the world, technologies like inflatable front and side airbags are allowing people to survive accidents which previously would have been fatal. While a lower fatality rate is in itself a good thing, the fact that more people survive results in more treatment of serious injuries to necks, torsos and legs.

The increased access to medical helicopters and improved medical procedures has also resulted in better survivability in serious accidents. But trauma care is costly and long-term chronic pain is often a result of automobile accidents, neither of which is particularly attractive to insurance companies who are stuck paying higher injury claims. The survivability of accidents has brought the focus onto building automotive structures and systems that not only keep people alive, but also lessen their injuries in the event of major collisions.

What Kills?

The top three lethal injuries in modern traffic accidents are interesting to consider. Brain injuries top the list. Such injuries occur when the head is stopped suddenly, but the brain, which is suspended in a fluid inside the head, continues forward and strikes the inside of the skull. As demonstrated by the recent deaths of several racing drivers, this kind of injury can occur even when the occupant is properly belted if the collision is severe enough or the initial speeds high enough. Brain injuries of this sort can cause nearly instantaneous death.

The second most common fatal injury occurs when the forward motion of the body stops and the heart continues traveling forward until it hits the abdominal cavity. This severe impact can be sufficient to actually rupture either the heart itself or tear the large aorta blood vessel from the heart. In either case the patient loses so much blood so quickly that death takes place in two or three minutes.

The third type of fatal injury in an automobile collision is a combination of injuries to two or more major organs, like the liver and spleen. These injuries can cause massive bleeding, although in some cases, if the patient can be transported quickly enough to a trauma center, the patient's life can be saved. What each of these fatal injuries has in common is that they result from a severe trauma to internal organs caused when the body stops suddenly and the internal organs don't.

What Seatbelts Do

Seatbelts have reduced fatalities in frontal collisions by 50 percent. The use of a seat belt and a frontal airbag improves survivability by another 10 percent. If you think these numbers aren't significant, consider than during the 1950s, the Air Force lost more pilots from car crashes than they did from airplane crashes. While those early jet-jockeys were notorious for their wild driving, the lack of seat belts in their cars made their driving more dangerous than their flying.

Aside from keeping the driver and passengers inside the car, seatbelts provide a way of dissipating the energy of the collision over time. Consider an automobile traveling at a constant 30-mph. If this automobile were to hit an immovable concrete barrier, it would come to a stop in about a tenth of a second. Modern cars are designed with deformable structures that crush progressively so that the vehicle would see a maximum deceleration of about 20-Gs, or twenty times the force of gravity. Now, let's put a driver in the car without a seat-belt. As the car strikes the concrete barrier and begins to decelerate, the driver continues forward at the same 30-mph until striking the relatively rigid steering wheel and steering column. Not that long ago these were highly rigid parts of the automobile but, more recently, they have become somewhat deformable and able to absorb some amount of impact energy. Much of the time and space for energy absorption has been used up by the driver flying through space, so when the driver's body finally stops it does so over a much shorter time. The driver stops moving in just a few hundredths of a second with a deceleration as high a 150-Gs. But that's just the outside of the body. Inside, the internal organs and brain continue forward, finally smashing into bones and skull with huge impacts that cause the fatal injuries mentioned earlier.

Now, let's put seatbelts on our driver. After some initial time to take up the slack in the belts, the driver is held by the belt and is allowed to decelerate at the same rate as the vehicle. Instead of with-standing 150-Gs, the driver may get hit with 40-G's of deceleration. This is uncomfortable, and may cause some injuries, but it should be survivable. Most people would consider a 30-mph crash to be fairly low speed, something they might be able to brace themselves against using their arms. But consider that a deceleration rate of 40-Gs means a 200 pound man, for example, would have to be able to bench press 40 times their body weight or more than 8,000 pounds to do the same job as the seat belts. To reduce injuries even further, some cars are now fitted with pyrotechnic pre-tensioners that take up the slack in the belts almost instantly and subject the driver to only the same 20-G forces that the car sees in our 30-mph crash. In these cases the seat belts reduce the g-force experienced by the brain and internal organs to easily survivable levels. The addition of a frontal airbag does the same thing as a seatbelt and was originally intended as a way to reduce injuries to people who refused to wear seatbelts. When used in conjunction with seatbelts they have the same effect as the pre-tensioner, allowing the driver or passenger to ride down the deceleration at the same rate as the vehicle.

Leg Injuries

With the upper torso well restrained by seat belts and airbags in frontal collisions, significant injuries to the legs are now more common. Actually these injuries were occurring before, but the upper torso injuries were frequently fatal, and therefore, the leg injuries were unimportant. As the front structure of an automobile deforms, absorbing the energy of the collision, major components like the engine and transmission and front wheels and suspension are moved back. If a car isn't carefully designed, these large heavy items can move into the passenger compartment causing injury to the lower legs and feet and possibly trapping the occupant in the car. Manufacturers are now designing special reinforcements at the rear of the front wheel arches and longitudinal load bearers that deflect the heavy components downward and away from the passenger compartment.

Side Impacts

In a side impact there is much less space to absorb the energy of a collision. The sides of the automobile must, therefore, be designed to distribute as much of the force as possible over the rest of the structure. In the Saab 9-3 and 9-5 models, for example, this is accomplished by making the B-pillar behind the front doors from very rigid high-strength steel so that it will not deform under the forces of a collision. Instead of deforming, the rigid B-pillar hinges inward from the top at the roof. This hinging or pivoting of the B-pillar means the upper part of the vehicle cabin receives little of the deformation while the lower part near the driver's pelvic area receives the most and absorbs the majority of the impact. A human's pelvis is much stronger and more resistant to damage than the rib cage, head and chest.

To further protect the vulnerable areas, side impact airbags are becoming more popular. In the best cases the airbag inflates in two stages. The first section inflates to protect the rib cage and internal organs. In the second stage the upper part of the airbag inflates to protect the head. In a side impact, the head often flops over to the side sometimes impacting the side window or even the hood of the intruding vehicle through the driver's window. A side impact airbag keeps the head upright and safe from these violent impacts.

When you think of the small amount of space available for deformation and how little time it takes for the impacting vehicle to cover that space, it is easy to see why side airbags must be designed to deploy quickly. The gas generator must trigger in as little as 5-thousandths of a second. The lower section of a two-stage side airbag deploys in about 15-thousanths of a second while the upper bag is in place about 30-thousandths of a second after the collision occurs.

Rear-end Collisions

While the fatality rates for rear-end collisions are much lower, they cause most of the long-term and chronic pain symptoms of accident victims. According to the Insurance Institute for Highway Safety, whiplash injuries from automobile accidents accounted for almost $7 billion in insurance payments in the US in 1997. Improper or ineffective seat head restraints are part of the problem and studies show only about ten percent of drivers have a properly adjusted headrest. Lear Corporation filed a US Patent in 1993 for an active head restraint system to overcome this problem. Their system minimizes head movement during a rear impact by a linkage that is connected between the headrest and a plate that is located in the seat back. The plate is pushed rearward by the body during a rear collision and this rearward motion is translated into an upward and forward motion by the headrest. After the collision, the plate in the seatback and the headrests automatically move back into their original position, with no damage to the seat. The Saab Active Head Restraint incorporated the Lear design into the Saab 9-5 models in 1997 and the Saab 9-3 in 1998. Other GM Models have followed suit.

Room for Improvement

While the goal of an injury-proof automobile is an unrealistic one, the progress that has been made in making cars safer in the past fifteen years is admirable. Some companies have been content to follow these developments (adding another airbag when the market demands it) others have been leaders in the science of making cars safer. Making safer cars is only half the equation. The real gains will come when we start teaching attentive driving and accident avoidance. These will reduce the possibility of accidents in the first place.

CHAPTER 14

British sports cars were made for weekends

What is it about old British sports cars that makes people love them? They aren't fast. Their lack of reliability is legendary. Even when they were new, they couldn't really be taken seriously as daily transportation. And today, they are far from new. The last MGB rolled off the assembly line more than 20 years ago. The classic E-Type Jaguar is more than 30 years old. Most people look at them as rolling antiques, quaint throwbacks but not serious automobiles.

Fortunately, all over the country there are groups of like-minded anglophiles whose life mission is to keep old British cars on the road; a hopeless adoration for the less than perfect products of the British automobile industry. The good news is that the British made a huge variety of highly impractical, but nevertheless charming, vehicles during the past 100 years. This was especially true during the period between 1945 and 1980 when the British sports car was discovered and loved by more than a few crazy Yanks.

The story is an old one, well worn through its telling and retelling. American GI's stationed in England during the war discovered the nimble handling and female-attracting abilities of small British sports cars. The Americans were the only ones who had the money to drive during the war. It was said by British soldiers that the biggest problem they faced with the American soldiers in England was that they were overpaid, oversexed and over here. The cars that most

Americans discovered were pre-war MG roadsters. After the war ended and our boys came marching home, they brought back a taste for the little cars they had been driving in England. The lads at the MG Car Company were quick to figure out that there was a market and started sending the spindly MG TC to America. The TC was right-hand drive and with 1250cc and little more than 50 horsepower; it was a strange choice for a country whose roads stretched from here to Kansas. Ultimately, that didn't matter and MG became the sports car that America loved first. It started on the right and left coasts, but, before long, even middle Americans learned to stop pointing and laughing when a sports car went by.

Eventually, Jaguar showed us what real performance was all about and the side curtains of Triumph TR3s and MGAs gave way to roll-up windows. There was a time during the mid-sixties when cars like the MGB, Triumph TR4, Austin Healey 3000 and Jaguar Mark II could actually be used as daily transportation. Meanwhile, hoping that Americans would value charm over substance, the British also sent us a series of mostly forgettable sedans. They were largely ignored, except for the truly exceptional Austin Mini and Mini Cooper. The shear brilliance of this tiny car overcame indifferent build quality and poor service to gain a small niche of British sedan enthusiasts. As the Mini was not officially imported after 1967, the number of Mini owners in America has always been very small, but the influence of the motorized shoebox has always been larger than its sales numbers would indicate.

The seventies were a sad time for British car enthusiasts in America. British cars began to disappear as the British auto industry killed them or allowed them to wither on the vine. The MGB and Midget and Triumph Spitfire were kept around far too long. The Triumph TR7 was never developed, Jaguar replaced the E-Type with a sedan-based coupe, sports cars were almost dead and the prevailing thought was that government regulations would soon prohibit such fun anyway. By the early eighties, the game was over and the British sports car in America was a fond memory.

Actually, the British sports car was more than a fond memory for the people at Mazda who copied all the best attributes and emotions of the British sports car and wrapped them up in a reliable Japanese car called the Miata. It was hugely successful and may have single-handedly brought the idea of sports cars in America back to life. Other companies followed and a whole generation of drivers has grown up thinking of the Miata, MR2, Boxster and Z-Roadsters as the only true affordable sports cars.

But wait. All through those decades of good and bad, the number of fans of the traditional British sports car has continued to grow. For a long time it was self-preservation: the only way to get parts for your old roadster was to know someone who knew someone who had a cache of spares. More recently, specialty companies are remanufacturing spares and you can buy them straight off the shelf or, more likely, through mail order. There has never been a better time to keep an old British car running and the parts availability is probably better now than it was when these cars were new.

What do owners of these old, slow and antiquated examples of British engineering and craftsmanship do with their cars? For one thing, they drive them. They drive them a lot. The Central Ohio MG Owners (COMGO) is a good example of a British sports car club with an impressive event schedule. They have driving tours. They go together to vintage races. They caravan on long trips to national MG meets. COMGO has several hundred members and most of them aren't afraid to drive their old cars over hundreds of miles.

Their first driving tour of the spring season was on a sunny but chilly morning and twenty nine cars showed up. The oldest was a pre-war MG SA sedan. The newest was a late model mini-van, driven by a club member whose MG restoration project wasn't finished yet. In between were an assortment of MG TCs and TDs from the late forties and early fifties, a few MGAs from the fifties, an MG Midget or two and a whole slew of MGBs. It seems like the MGB is the car you drive on a long trip when you don't want to take out your hard-riding T-Type. Some of the MGBs were converted to MGB-V8 configuration. In the early seventies the factory made a few cars with the Rover aluminum V-8 engine. In the best of American hot-rodding traditions, a fair number of MG owners have converted their MGBs into V-8s. Most car clubs would look askance at such sacrilege but, because the factory did it first, it seems somehow okay amongst the MG brethren.

The driving tour started at 9:30 on a Saturday morning and was covered 250 miles of southern Ohio scenery. Contrary to what most people who only drive on Ohio Interstates think, the state is not all flat highways blanketed with state trooper radar. In fact, the southern and central part of the state is mostly rolling farmland, intersected by pretty streams and rivers. In other words, *sports car country*. The tour was just that and there were no checkpoints or set speeds. Several of the owners of the T-Types, including me in my vintage-racerized MG TD, chose to make it a leisurely drive, letting the faster MGBs and Midgets roar by when they came upon us.

Driving a T-Type MG on a trip has to be approached in the right frame of mind. If you are concerned with how soon or even if you will be arriving, then you are not in the right frame of mind. These cars are 50 years old and were designed to be driven on the winding lanes surrounding Oxford and Abingdon in England. They are great fun for puttering along at 45-50-mph. They are not great fun on any Interstate highway above 60-mph.

The best part about driving an open car through the countryside is the variety of smells that come wafting by. Fresh cut grass, cow manure, haystacks and hot asphalt all have their own aromas that you just don't notice when you are rushing along in an air conditioned modern car. You have to actually drive these cars. More than anything else you feel like you are flying in a biplane. The engines are tiny and not very powerful, so lots of shifting is required to keep up with traffic. The noises they make say *sports car*. People wave at you from their front porch and most look a little bit envious. If you squint just right you can pretend that it is 1955.

For lunch, the MGs took over the fast food restaurants in a small town. All of the MG T-Type owners grouped together for a leisurely lunch, punctuated by discussions about their cars. When we left, you could tell where each T-Type had been by the little puddle of oil it had left behind. By the end of the day, as we all pulled into a local tavern for a pre-arranged dinner, I was tired. My face was wind-burned from the day outdoors. I had forgotten how exposed you are at 45-mph in a sports car without a windshield. We take so much for granted on modern cars. My legs were slightly cramped and my butt was sore from eight hours in the saddle. Our group of T-types had had a pretty trouble-free day. The fan on my engine had chosen this opportunity to shed a blade, but it was an easy matter of wrenching four bolts to remove the entire fan and drive without it. It always helps to bring a few wrenches along with you when you drive an old car. Other than that, for a group of cars more than fifty years old, covering the 250-mile drive had been a stress-free day.

Another thing that British car owners do with their cars is show them off. The British Car Council of Central Ohio coordinates the events and efforts of the various car clubs in and around the Columbus, Ohio area. For twenty-two years the Council has organized a show for owners of British cars and motorcycles. The last couple of years the show has taken place at Easton Town Center, a group of upscale shopping malls in the suburb of Easton. Somewhere between 300 and 350 cars show up to this event and the variety is impressive. There were the expected MGs, Triumphs and Austin Healeys. There were Jaguars and Land Rovers and Mini Coopers. There were Sunbeams and Morgans and the odd TVR. The cars were arranged by marque in different parts of the outdoor mall and literally thousands of people wandered around to look at the cars. Some of the cars were polished and pampered to concours perfection. Most were well-cared-for examples that are driven on weekends. A few were ratty old sports cars, held together by bailing wire and hope as they visited their appointed rounds. More than a few were for sale, as their owners were ready to move onto another project or up to another automotive dream. The crowd at Easton was typically friendly mid-western in its makeup and everyone was there to have a good time.

The owners of these British cars are interesting. Many brought lawn chairs and beach umbrellas and spent the day sitting next to their cars and comparing stories about their automotive passions. Some take it all very seriously, preparing their cars for judging by the other participants. Most are there to talk about cars and see people they only see when they indulge in their car hobby. There are plenty of older owners, but also a good mix of middle-aged and younger owners, too. This is important. As the cars get older there is a real danger that the people who connect with them will grow too old to enjoy them any longer. This has happened to Model T and Model A Fords and to a certain extent it is happening to T-Type MGs. People who are at an age where they have disposable income for a collector car, are more likely to buy a muscle car that reminds them of their youth, rather than an old, slow MG from their parents' era. As the population ages, the number of enthusiasts for old British sports cars may diminish, eventually causing a decline in interest. That would be a pity. Unless you have experienced the responsiveness, driving characteristics and even the hardship of an old British sports car, you can't really appreciate what we have gained, and also what we have lost, in our modern cars. Fortunately, the enthusiasm of youthful owners and the large crowd at the Easton British Car Show gives hope that the interest in old British sports cars will remain high for many years to come.

CHAPTER 15

Half Life:
Forever is a long time

While sitting in the paddock of a vintage race, an attractive woman walked by and stopped to admire my 1952 MG TD. I was pleased she took an interest in my car and I tried to explain how much I enjoy racing a car that is so painfully slow. I was happy with our conversation until she asked me how long it took to fully restore a car to perfection. I thought for a moment and realized the answer wouldn't please her. "Forever."

It takes forever to make everything perfect. I am pretty sure she would have rather heard a more reasonable "year or two" as a response, but that answer would have been far less truthful than the glib answer I had given her.

Shortly after the turn of the century, about the same time the automobile was becoming a locomotion force worthy of reckoning, physicists started to understand radioactivity. Of intense interest was the concept of radioactive decay, the idea that a radioactive material would gradually lose a portion of its strength over time. They coined the term half-life to describe the time it took for a given material to fall to one-half its original radioactive strength. Different materials have different half-lives and by measuring the strength of minute quantities of radioactivity found with artifacts, it became possible to date ancient ruins and structures with reasonable accuracy. The concept of half-life found its way into other scientific fields, particularly biology, where growth and decay of organisms could be modeled in the same way as radioactivity.

An automobile, even a simple automobile from the 1950s, is made up of literally thousands of small and large individual parts. Bolts, nuts, washers, screws, rivets, brackets, pipes, hoses, fluids, gears, belts, pulleys, castings and forgings are all combined into larger assemblies that eventually combine to become a vehicle. When you set about restoring a vehicle, the object is to disassemble, renovate and repair as many of the sub-systems that you possibly can. In a very thorough job, nearly every single nut and bolt of every system is taken apart and examined. Most experienced restorers work methodically, system by system, setting aside the finished part until all of the systems are ready to go back together to make a car.

But that is where the concept of a half-life begins to haunt. As soon as a system has been assembled, its clock begins ticking. It is only a matter of time before its perfection, and, therefore, its performance, begins to degrade. And some systems degrade faster than others. I am pretty sure, for example, that the Lucas electrical systems found on most fifties and sixties British sports cars began their countdown at the same moment they were produced at the Lucas factory. Shipping the parts to the car maker further shortened the usable life, as did transporting the car over the Atlantic to the States. All of this took valuable time. By the time a happy new sports car owner took delivery, half the life of the electrics had probably already spilled out.

It is also quite possible to dramatically shorten the natural half-life of some components. British braking systems are notoriously unforgiving of anything but Castrol LMA brake fluid. Put in bargain basement fluid from the corner auto parts store and the internal timer for the system jumps into hyperspace. The brake job you thought you might do next year will be required within the next month. You don't believe it? Try putting some generic brake fluid in your clutch master cylinder and see how long it will be before you are learning how to drive without a clutch. We are messing with natural forces here that are far beyond our understanding.

Oddly enough, the cars from different countries can have dramatically different half-lives. German cars have a reputation for lasting nearly forever. Each system has the Teutonic good sense to maintain its integrity as long as each of the other systems. There is a tradition of keeping cars for a long time in Germany and the cars are simply expected to last a long time. The British keep their cars a long time, too, but are much more tolerant of individual system failures. Swedish cars are much like German ones; who wants to get stuck far from home in the middle of a Swedish winter? The bodies of French cars seem to far outlast their mechanical components, while Italian cars are decidedly the opposite. Each of these countries is geographically close to the others, yet each has its own half-life quirks.

Which brings me back to my cynical, if depressingly truthful, answer about restoring an old car. As soon as you have started the process, the clock begins ticking. Even sitting on a shelf waiting to go into the car, metal is exposed to air, seals are deprived of necessary lubrication, rubber is aging and hardening and things have begun to slowly slide downhill. By the time the car itself has gone together, part of its life has already ebbed away.

Okay, so you are willing to put up with the small degradation and pronounce the car perfect at the end of its restoration. How long will it last that way? Weeks? Days? Hours? Seconds? For some, especially those in the concours set, the answer is never to drive the car, but to cart it from car show to car show in a hermetically sealed trailer. It doesn't matter; the clock is still silently ticking. But there is a better way. *Drive the hell out of the car.* Sure you will speed up the decay process, but long before the car reaches its half-life you will have driven it and enjoyed it far more than you enjoyed pulling it around on a trailer. The key is to cram as many miles into the car's half-life as you possibly can.

If you vintage race your old car, it's even better, because others get to watch you enjoying your old car. The natural decay process is dramatically accelerated for cars that are used on a racetrack. Everything gets stressed far more than street driving levels. But the miles you put on before the half-life is reached are some of the most exciting you can imagine. At some point, when your restored car has reached its half-life, you will discover it has attained an honorable patina of age and competition that can't be duplicated by any restoration shop. At this point, individual components and systems are replaced as needed, but the car itself needs to be preserved as a tribute to its and your own illustrious history.

So perfection can never be attained and it literally would take forever to restore a car to its highest level. But that isn't or shouldn't be a goal. My cars have stone chips and small dings and scuffs that come from everyday use and the occasional racetrack foray. I am happy with that. Besides, forever is way too long to spend working on a car.

CHAPTER 16

Special Delivery:
Getting from there to here

Southern cars don't rust. Everybody knows that. When you live in the buckle of the rustbelt and are looking to buy an old car, you look South. While Florida has its beaches and salt air, Missouri its Mississippi River floods and Arizona its dash-cracking heat, none of those states dump tons of iron-eating salt on their roadways like those of the Midwest. Cars from California, the South and Southwestern states always bring a premium.

The Internet has made it pretty easy to find cars in far away states, but there are obvious problems associated with buying a car in California when you live in Michigan. Short of actually traveling across the country to look at the vehicle in question, at some point you are going to have to trust that the dealer or owner is telling the truth about its mechanical and physical condition. One person's idea of a show car might be a horror to you. Pictures help, of course, but ultimately, unless you can have the car independently appraised or can afford the time and airfare, you will be at somebody's mercy.

The second problem—getting payment to the owner—is much easier than it used to be. But before any money leaves your pocket, have a copy of the vehicle's title faxed or overnight mailed to you. You want to be sure that the owner has the right to sell you the vehicle and that it hasn't been stolen. The title is no guarantee, but at least it is an indication that everything is on the up and up. Most owners want to have a certified bank check sent to them, but an easier way is a direct electronic money transfer from your bank to theirs. You will need their account number and the electronic routing code for their bank. The money usually gets transferred within about half a day. On the other hand, if they ask you to send money to Nigeria, you might want to think twice about the whole deal.

Now that you own your car, how do you get it home? There are a lot of people who are in business to help you do just that. Car transport companies can range from an individual with an open trailer and a pickup truck to one of the big national companies that haul eight to twelve cars at a time in enclosed trailers. Smaller operators tend to deliver more quickly and keep the car on the trailer until it is delivered. Larger companies sometimes move the car from location to location as freight demands.

The kind of service you want depends upon what kind of car you are moving and what kind of budget you have. A convertible or pre-war car is better off enclosed. More modern cars and hardtops are usually fine on an exposed open trailer. Prices are usually pretty consistent: $800-$1200 for an open trailer from the West coast to the Midwest with a closed trailer costing $1200 to $1800. Winter months can cost more and take longer. Most companies also charge more for cars that aren't running, or spare parts that are also along for the ride.

There is another option to hiring a transporter, one that is hard to recommend although I have done it myself on many occasions: You can fly to the city in question, meet the owner in person and drive the car back home again. This can be a wonderful experience and opportunity to bond with your new purchase, or it can be an exercise in frustration and despair as you sit broken down along the side of the highway, awaiting the tow truck's arrival. The following three stories will illustrate how things can go wrong in a hurry and what to do about it.

I bought a Land Rover Series IIA. It was a charming old vehicle, somewhat worse for wear and living in Maryland. The price seemed too good to be true. It was. I flew to Philadelphia and had the owner pick me up at the airport. We drove to his home as he told me in glowing terms how great the old Series IIA was. When we pulled into his driveway, my heart sank. It looked pretty rough. A quick check of the important parts, like brakes, lights and wipers, confirmed that everything worked. I paid my money and hit the road.

An hour later (about 45 miles at the Land Rover's leisurely pace) I noticed the oil pressure was beginning to drop. About the same moment, it began to snow. By now I was getting pretty weary of the combination of tire noise and gear whine that characterizes any trip in an old Land Rover. By chance, I also happened to be driving past a national truck and trailer rental outlet. I wheeled the Land Rover in and a half-hour later was underway with a moving truck towing a car trailer with my Land Rover strapped to it. The cost for a one-way rental was $900, about what it would have cost to have the vehicle shipped on a trailer from Maryland to Michigan. Add in the airfare and the better choice becomes clear. When I got home, I discovered the dropping oil pressure was due to a faulty gauge and the Land Rover's engine was fine.

I bought a 1967 Mercedes-Benz 250SE Coupe in Dallas, Texas. The owner told me it had a new interior and paint job and that the engine had less than 1000 miles on a rebuild. I contacted the repair shop that did the work and they confirmed the car to be in excellent mechanical condition. I flew to Dallas with a cashier's check and we did our transaction in the airport parking lot. I drove away listening to the sweet purr of the fuel-injected inline six-cylinder engine, and 20 hours later, as I pulled into my driveway, the sound was still as sweet. My only moment of hesitation on the entire trip was at

9:00 p.m. in East St. Louis, when the ammeter flickered a bit, causing the headlights to dim. This would have been a bad place to have car trouble but, after a moment, things settled down again and the trip went without incident. Best of all, I now feel a real affinity toward this car, having trusted it to bring me safely home. Mercedes-Benz has a reputation for building solid, reliable cars and experiences like this help keep that reputation alive.

Italian cars are not particularly known for being solid nor reliable. That's why when my friend Larry invited me to fly to Phoenix to drive his thirty-one-year-old Ferrari back to Ann Arbor in December, I hesitated for a second or two before saying yes. Larry owned this particular 1967 Ferrari 330GT2+2 once before, and has talked about its greatness ever since. It is an unusual shade of light blue with dark blue leather upholstery a striking and beautiful combination. It is one of the last twenty cars built in that series and is powered by a lusty 330 horsepower V-12 engine. The previous owner lived in Tucson and had recently rewired the entire car and had the carburetors rebuilt. The car certainly looked impressive as Larry rolled up to the curb of the Phoenix Sky Harbor, just across from the taxi stand, on a pleasant early afternoon.

The warm and sunny skies of Phoenix gave way to overcast as we headed north out of town. By Flagstaff, the temperature had dropped to the low twenties and it was snowing. It was then that we discovered that the heater on the Ferrari didn't work. Who ever heard of a Ferrari that doesn't fry your feet as you drive? Warm water was traveling through the heater hoses, but apparently the Tucson owner, tired of roasting while driving, managed to disable the flow of any warm air into the cockpit. In December, in a snowstorm in Flagstaff, that little modification meant numb toes and significant shivering. We had also discovered another irritation. The driveline had a severe vibration that seemed to be strongest right around 70-mph. It smoothed out a bit between 90 and 100-mph, so we adopted that as our cruising speed. But the noise caused by the vibration and the air rushing past thirty-year-old window seals made conversation nearly impossible.

Driving an old car across country is often an exercise in crisis management. Just as you adapt to one problem, another crops up to vie for your attention. Late in the afternoon, we noticed the ammeter gauge was showing no charge from the alternator. It didn't seem so bad as long as we drove quickly, but when night came and we turned on the headlights, the discharge was severe and we stopped early for the night. With ears ringing from the noise and feet frozen from the cold, we looked for the address of a local electrical shop. The next morning we arrived at 7:30 am and waited until the owner arrived at 9:00 am. He quickly set to work with his diagnostic tools and told us that there was nothing wrong with our alternator. He did find a slightly loose connection on the main battery cable and $20 later we were on the road again, confident that he had found the problem.

Twenty miles later, the ammeter began to show discharge and it was clear the problem still remained. Our solution was simple: We bought a spare battery and a small battery charger. In spite of the problems, we were enjoying driving the Italian thoroughbred across America. People waved and when we stopped a crowd would gather and peer into the engine bay as we checked the oil and fluids. All day long we boomed along in the big blue Ferrari, trying to make as much time as we could, knowing that our battery would only last a short way into the night before it ran down. Evening came. How long would we be able to drive just on battery power? The answer came about an hour an a half later. Suddenly the lights dimmed and the car started to stutter as we rolled to a stop at the top of a handy exit ramp. Ten minutes later, new battery installed, we were rolling again, heading-on toward Oklahoma City.

Our plan had been to drive all day and half the night. With the charging problems, we weren't able to drive late into the evenings and the distance to home still seemed way too far. That evening, we parked the Ferrari near the hotel pool and used an electrical outlet to charge the battery in the car. Then, overnight, we charged the other battery in our room. The local television told of a major winter storm just to the south and we vowed to be on the road early and drive as far and as fast as we could on the first battery, before switching to the second. At dawn we stopped for breakfast and changed the now dead battery.

Without the drain of the headlights, we expected the second battery would last most of the day. Two hours later, we were shocked to feel the now-familiar miss as the ignition no longer had enough juice to keep the big twelve-cylinder engine running. Apparently the deeply discharged batteries needed more than the small charger could provide at night. We glided to a stop in a fast-food gas station and pondered our fate. Gas stations used to be places of salvation for stranded motorists. Now they sell pork rinds, corn nuts and soda and the clerks look at you blankly when you ask about actual automotive service. Larry started walking for town in search of another battery, while I waited with the car. After a while, a local in a Chevelle SS396 convertible drove up and admired the car. We talked about our problems and he suggested we try J&A Automotive a local repair shop that ships its rebuilt components all over the country. Larry returned with the battery and we headed into Marshfield, Missouri, in search of electronic salvation.

Ferraris use a Magnetti Marelli alternator and regulator system. The guys at J&A had rebuilt Marelli alternators before, but didn't have the parts for this one. What they did have was a Nippon Denso alternator for a Japanese car which fit the existing brackets perfectly. Less than an hour and a half after rolling to a stop with a dead battery and little hope, we were on the road again, the ammeter now

103

showing a healthy level of charge. The sun came out and for a brief time we were even able to remove some layers of clothing without freezing. The rest of the day and into the night we hammered the Ferrari, finally arriving home shortly before midnight, alternator still producing a good charge. For the next two days my ears were still ringing from the noise and vibration, but the trip was one I will always remember.

Having done several long distance drives in newly purchased old cars, there are some things you should bring with you. The most important tool you can carry in an old car is a cellular telephone. If things get really bad, you can always call for help. An auto club card and a credit card are next on the list. I hardly ever travel without my Swiss Army knife and I like to bring a pair of pliers, a couple of assorted screw drivers, duct tape and some strong wire along on any old car trip. A small battery charger is also a good bet, with an extension cord so that you can shore up a balky electrical system with overnight charges. Don't forget a couple of good strong flashlights and a couple of road flares or triangles and a small fire extinguisher for safety. Most of these items can fit into a cloth tool roll that is easy to carry. Someday maybe I'll actually make a trip with all of these vital items. Mostly, I just make due with what I can find along the way.

Trips like these stick in our memory and add to an appreciation for what driving used to be like. Modern cars are wonders of reliability, performance and refinement. Old cars have character and, sometimes, build character. About halfway through the trip from Phoenix, Larry commented that had we been driving a Honda, we probably would have been home already. I reminded Larry that had it been a Honda instead of a Ferrari, I probably wouldn't have flown to Phoenix to make the trip. Adventure is all around us, and driving anyplace in an old car is always an adventure.

CHAPTER 17

Where Has All The Steering Gone?
Progress always leaves something behind

Only a Luddite wouldn't agree that today's cars are better than they have ever been. Advances in every area of technology and design have produced innovations that weren't even dreamed of by our automotive forefathers. Cars are aerodynamic and fuel-efficient, comfortable and environmentally friendly, and have better cornering capability than all-out racing cars from just a few years ago. If the cars of fifty and sixty years ago were more stylish—a subjective call—the latest trend is bringing some of that retro-look back in a modern package. If this were a perfect world, that could be the end of the story. But like our world, progress isn't perfect. Even when it results in dramatic improvements, progress always leaves something behind.

Years ago, all cars had tall skinny tires. These tires had rounded cross-sections that resulted in a tire footprint on the ground that was longer than it was wide. This footprint shape was highly effective at holding a straight line, as any small motion away from center would create a self-aligning torque that pulled the tire straight again. To move it away from straight ahead required significant effort at the steering wheel to overcome this self-aligning torque. To a driver, this directional stability meant a car was easy to drive at high speed. Early radial tires from European tire makers like Dunlop, Michelin and Pirelli, with highly rounded crowns were especially appreciated for this characteristic. Sports car builders like Jaguar, Mercedes-Benz,

Ferrari and Aston Martin knew how to take advantage of directional stability to create cars with legendary steering feel. Even lower-cost sports cars like the MGB or Austin Healey 3000 exhibited wonderfully precise high-speed road manners. Engineers from Saab, Volvo and BMW understood the concepts and applied them to sedans that are now remembered for their steering excellence.

It all began to change in the 1970's. Racing cars had moved away from tires with tread grooves to slick tires. Because of extremely high levels of horsepower, these tires needed to be very wide to provide driving traction. Racing cars have highly adjustable suspensions, so wide tires could also be used on the front wheels and the alignment set to take advantage of the performance levels. Racing cars of this and almost every other period are designed to operate strictly at their limits of performance. Most are not very pleasant to operate when driven slowly. Everything is sacrificed for predictable performance at the tire limits. Racing cars dart and weave and seem uncoordinated at low speeds and only settle down as their limits are approached. This is the opposite of what one wants in a street-driven car, especially a sports car. But because the racing look included wide tires and flared fenders, the street performance market developed along the same lines. Enthusiasts fell for the idea that wide tires were better for handling and performance.

In fact, they aren't. As a tire gets wider, its contact footprint also gets shorter, leaving less opportunity for a build-up of self-aligning torque. In addition, wide tires need to stay square to the ground to produce maximum cornering. This can be accomplished with a highly adjustable suspension on a racing car with little suspension travel, but is nearly impossible to attain on a car that must absorb bumps and potholes on the street. None of that mattered: style dictated fat tires no matter how they might adversely affect handling. Paradoxically, the result of placing excessively wide tires on inap-

106

propriate street-driven performance cars was accepted as a *de facto* characteristic of high performance driving. Cars with skinny tires and superb steering like the mid-1980s Mercedes-Benz 300E Sedans lost their edge, wandered at high speed and became darty at low speeds with the application of wide performance tires. The ultimate levels of grip on a racetrack might have been higher, but the handling characteristics when driven on the street suffered.

By the late 1980's, car manufacturers were following the lead of the aftermarket by offering wide tires on their performance models. Engineers at tire companies and car manufacturers struggled to find suspension setups that would give back what had been lost in steering feel and directional stability. Some, like BMW and Porsche were more successful than most, but their efforts were still not on par with average cars of previous decades. Meanwhile, power steering became popular, even on sports sedans, and proper steering feel has been relegated to distant memories.

Today, although suspension systems have been refined to take more advantage of wider tires, the trend has been to larger wheel diameters with lower tire aspect ratios. The aspect ratio is the ratio of the tire sidewall height to the overall tire diameter. So even though the wheels are getting bigger in diameter, lower aspect ratios mean the overall diameter is staying the same. Fine on the racetrack where ultimate grip is king, but on the street the end result of this misdirected technology is even shorter tire contact footprints that further degrade steering feel and directional stability. For street usage, tires of 17, 18, or even 20-inch wheel diameters are actually detrimental to good handling, yet enthusiasts demand them, tire manufacturers produce them and car makers put them on sport models and show cars that represent the extreme edge of vehicle performance. It's a fantasy based upon how fat, low aspect ratio tires look under bulging wheel wells, rather than the actual vehicle dynamics.

Unfortunately, the trend shows every sign of continuing. First, the gradual deterioration of steering quality means that only a small number of today's automotive engineers have ever experienced how good it can be. They look perplexed when you complain about something they have just been praising. Second, the visual image that most performance stylists are emulating is still based upon racing, mostly Touring Sedans from Europe and Asia. These racers use ultra-low profile 17 and 18-inch tires, so "hot" street cars require the same size rubber. Lastly, it is clear that technological progress has made the modern automobile a remarkable device, so anyone who suggests otherwise is viewed as nostalgic and someone who will be left behind.

CHAPTER 18

That Will Teach You:
Skinned knuckles and the art of education

We aren't doing a very good job of educating our youth. I'm not talking about whether Johnny can read, or declining scores on standardized testing. Those are vital matters that politicians bring up before elections. The lack of education I decry is the automotive variety, and it came about when they closed down the school of hard knocks.

When was the last time you changed a set of spark plugs? Changed your own oil? Checked the fluid in the transmission or brake master cylinder? Even those of us who like cars hardly ever do that anymore. What's more, cars of the past decade have become so complicated and yet reliable they don't need much maintenance. When they do, it is far easier and more cost effective to take them to a certified mechanic than it is to get our hands dirty ourselves. So when a teenager gets a ten-year old beater to drive to school and job, it's likely to be reliable and trouble free, teaching them exactly nothing. It wasn't always like this.

A Coming of Age

Cars used to be finicky, temperamental devices, especially "beater" cars in the low price range. To keep them on the road required a basic understanding of how they worked and a modicum of skill with a wrench and pliers. Fouled plugs, stuck carburetor

109

chokes, clogged fuel filters, broken fan belts and worn brake linings were dealt with as they happened. As inconvenient as all this was, it taught generations of drivers to be more self-sufficient and capable of dealing with minor problems as they came along. Unreliable cars also taught people to find solutions to big problems when their cars died and left them stranded along the side of the highway. How you handled a breakdown on the highway said much about the person you were or would someday become.

As older cars have become more play toys than serious transportation, they get driven less and less. The reason for this is often a fear that they will break down and leave you stranded far from home. But as inconvenient as such an occurrence may be, is it always such a bad thing?

Learning New Skills

Changing a water pump or replacing brake pads will definitely teach you mechanical skills. But the most important things to learn from a breakdown on the road may have nothing to do with vise grips and screwdrivers. It can teach you how to manage an immediate problem, and these are skills that can translate into other parts of your life. Faced with a breakdown, you have to triage the situation. First, what are the symptoms? Next, what is a likely cause for such symptoms? Then, has the problem caused any secondary problems? Finally comes the question of repairing the breakdown. There are three possibilities here: you can fix it with what you have with, you can fix it if you can get the parts, or you can't fix it and need to tow or transport the car. Let's look at each scenario in more detail.

Bring Some Stuff

Even if you hardly ever hold a screwdriver, if you have a few basic tools along you can probably fix some of the things that can go wrong on the road. Some companies sell road emergency tool kits, but for the same money you can go to a hardware store and put together a better selection. Get a couple of screwdrivers, both standard and Phillips. Make one of the standard screwdrivers a fairly large one that you can also use to pry things apart or hold tension on the alternator while you replace a fan belt. Next, get a big pair of pliers, a pair of needle nose pliers and a pair of vise grips. Real mechanics will be aghast at the suggestion to use pliers or vise grips on bolts (they prefer only wrenches) but sometimes at the side of the road you have to improvise, and pliers can help. Wrenches are pretty useful things, too; and a set of inexpensive metric wrenches in their own holder will come in handy. The same goes for a small hammer, useful to tap grease caps back onto a hub after changing a wheel bearing or to hit a wrench to free a stubborn bolt. All of these tools can be kept in a small tool roll or bag that can also be found at a hardware store.

Jumper cables are another useful item to have. Just be aware that if you have them you will probably be asked to jump other people's cars far more than you will ever get yours jumped. Read the instructions carefully because you can really mess things up if you hook the cables up incorrectly. I always carry a roll of duct tape and some wire to make quick repairs if something is falling off. Bailing wire is just a soft steel wire that can be bent into place to hold up a muffler or keep a hood shut. I usually bring a handful of assorted plastic cable wrap ties with me because they are quick to attach and can hold out against amazing amounts of force. Throw in a can of flat fix, a good flashlight, some gloves to grab a hot exhaust pipe and an emergency triangle to alert other motorists and you have the makings of a first class emergency kit.

Parts is Parts

Fine, you have all the tools, but what if something has worn out

---

111

or broken? Each car has its Achilles heel, but some problems are common to most cars. If you bring a spare fan belt, a spare upper and lower radiator hose, a length of generic heater hose and some clamps, a few spare light bulbs and fuses and a spare wiper blade you will be able to fix most of the things that will ever go wrong. If your car never receives any maintenance and is on its last legs, you might bring a spare water pump, a couple quarts of engine oil, some radiator stop-leak and a new set of front wheel bearings. These are all larger jobs to repair, but even if you have to go to a garage, at least you will already have the parts they are going to need. Sometimes, if you can limp the car to the next town or take a taxi, you can find an auto parts store that will have the parts you need. But breakdowns always occur on a Sunday evening when everything is closed. You are better off if you are self-sufficient.

Tow

The last resort is getting towed. Sometimes this is impossible to avoid. But think carefully before agreeing to let the tow-truck operator take you to some impound lot on the far side of town. If your car is still being made by a recognized manufacturer, then have it taken to the local dealership. If that isn't an option, look in the Yellow Pages and find a foreign repair shop that at least lists your car in their advertisement. Even if it is a Sunday night, you can probably leave your car in their parking lot with a note that you will be back first thing in the morning. Find a hotel nearby if you can and get enough sleep so you will be ready for the trying day ahead of you.

There is an alternative to being at the mercy of the tow truck operator and unfamiliar mechanics. You can rent a truck and either a car trailer or tow dolly one way and do it yourself. First of all, you avoid the towing costs. Second, you can finish your trip with much less delay. Last, when you bring your car home, you can bring it to your own mechanic who is probably used to your eccentricities in vehicle choices and won't laugh nearly as hard when you show up with a dead car. Towing becomes part of the learning experience, too. Between military service and sheer necessity, most of our fathers and grandfathers knew how to tow a trailer. They knew that not having enough weight on the tongue would make the trailer sway and that the lights on a trailer almost never work the first time you hook them up. Maybe kids brought up on a farm still understand these basic facts, but it seems few city and suburban kids have a clue about the sizes of trailer hitch balls and which way the trailer will go when they turn the wheel while backing up. Just another one of those lessons that help make the fabric of our society stronger. Besides, there is a basic feeling of satisfaction in getting yourself out of a jam without the help of others.

Risk-taking

An unwillingness to take risks deprives you of the opportunity to test your limits. Few people look forward to a breakdown on the road. It can be unpleasant, but it can teach you about yourself, your strengths and your ability to cope with adversity. You can take the safe route and avoid such lessons by always driving new reliable cars. Or, you can embrace the character-building experience of something older and out of the ordinary. Don't let fear stop you. Think of it as enrolling in Hard Knocks 101.

CHAPTER 19

Car Lust:
When you are fifteen, anything seems possible

They say that men of today are interested in collecting the cars from their youth, that point in puberty when short skirts, tight jeans and pliable curves met chrome and shiny paint and the chest-pounding roar of a high performance engine. This explains the current strength of the muscle car market. Men with enough disposable income to purchase a collector car tend to be in their late forties through early sixties.

These men were around fifteen in 1964, when the muscle car era was just beginning. The Mustang had just been introduced, Pontiac's GTO was boss and the Camaro a couple of years away. Although those cars were made in great numbers in subsequent years, any classic car auctioneer will tell you that today those cars are money in the bank at US auctions. Corvettes from this period are also strong sellers and it is no coincidence that the most popular kit car design of all time is a replica of Carroll Shelby's AC Cobra.

It wasn't just American muscle that was popular then. The Jaguar E-type evokes the same sensual and openly sexual appeal it has always enjoyed. The MGB and Triumph TR4 and Porsche 911 all date from that same period in the mid-sixties. Each is highly sought after by baby-boomers who remember the cars sitting in the high school parking lot or cruising main street or running in the local autocross. The Triumph Spitfire and GT-6 and the MG Midget are lower price alternatives whose virtues of simplicity and low cost are being re-discovered thirty or forty years after they were made.

Ironically, even by the mid-sixties, the guys who had started the whole car enthusiast thing were being left behind. Kids, coming back from the war in 1945 at age 20, had started both the hotrod and sports car movements. Twenty years later, the cars they were interested in, the ones from their youth, the ones they wanted to collect, were pre-war models whose performance, braking ability and road-holding were far below the average family car of the day. Even worse, the sports cars they had raced in the early fifties, the ubiquitous MG TC and MG TD, the Allard and the early Porsches, were completely outclassed by even the cheapest mass-produced sports car or coupe. By 1970, the collector car hobby was dominated by people with Model T and Model A Fords who enjoyed the relaxed pace their cars could provide them.

I turned fifteen in 1972. By then it wasn't just rich kids who could afford a muscle car. The parking lot of Dixie Hollins High School in St. Petersburg, Florida was filled with flame-belching jacked-up, mid-sixties Mustangs and Camaros painted in a variety of candy-apple hues never imagined by Ford and Chevrolet's marketing managers. Slicks, traction bars, really huge hood scoops and chromed side exhausts let everyone know that this was a serious runner. But something had changed and a bad ride wasn't all that mattered. Kids graduated from high school and went off to die in Vietnam. Terrorists took hostages at the Olympics. Drug use hit our generation. Gas lines formed during the first oil embargo and everyone wanted to know what the President knew and when he knew it. We had lost our innocence, but we still liked cars.

My mother took my sister and me to Germany in 1972 to visit my grandmother near Wiesbaden. I was already immersed into foreign cars by this time, from the succession of Borgwards and Taunuses and others that my father brought home and nursed back to, if not health, at least mobility. Upon arriving in Germany, the first thing I did was hit the news stand and buy a car magazine. It was *Auto Motor Und Sport*, and it was their annual new car review issue. I poured over it daily, comparing the vital statistics of cars like the Swiss-built Monteverdi with the Italian-made Iso. Being an American, I knew acceleration was king when it came to performance and so I paid special attention to the 0-100 KPH (0-62 mph) numbers.

Just up the street from my grandmother's house, in a little village called Dotzheim, there was an Alfa Romeo dealership. I knew something about Alfas because they would come to race at Daytona and Sebring in my home state and I followed the newspaper reports of those two classic races. In the front window of the Dotzheim Alfa dealership was an angular coupe whose half-lidded headlamps and aggressive snout spoke of a whole new world of exotic performance. I rushed home and searched my magazine until I found it. An Alfa Romeo Montreal. The name was so exotic! It was powered by a V-8 engine, just like so many of those Mustangs and Camaros. But this was a four-cam V-8 in aluminum. I couldn't imagine anything so advanced. It was fast and powerful and to my young eyes, indescribably beautiful like Leslie Caron in *Father Goose* or Sophia Loren in an evening dress. A 15-year old's lust.

One day, while leafing through my *Auto Motor Und Sport*, I stumbled across a company called Lotus. Their cars were tiny, almost toy-like. One caught my eye for the sheer simplicity of it. Colin Chapman designed the Lotus Seven to be about as minimal as a sports car could possibly be. Nothing on the car was there to do anything but make it faster. And it was fast. With a simple, rudimentary engine, the Seven was one of the quickest cars in my well-worn magazine. It looked vaguely pre-war with a flat grille, open fenders and stand-alone head-lamps. It was cheeky and funny and appealing all at the same time.

116

If the Alfa had been Sophia Loren, the Lotus Seven was more like Liza Minnelli in *Cabaret*; open and brash, a car to make you laugh. I had a new favorite.

It would be years before I actually got to see a Lotus Seven for real. I went to college in upstate New York. Bob, one of my friends from the campus sports car club, lived in Marblehead, Massachusetts, a beautiful seacoast town not far from Boston. We went for a long drive one morning and ended up that afternoon in Marblehead. We headed over to DSK Cars, a company that built updated versions of Colin Chapman's original Lotus Seven design. The shop was located in the building that Ray Caldwell used to use to build his Autodynamics Formula Vees and Formula Fords. The guys at DSK were very kind to a couple of college kids, letting us sit in several prototypes and explaining all the improvements they had made. Sitting in the car renewed my lust and I knew I would eventually own a Lotus Seven.

I kept my eyes open. Everywhere I went, I looked for old Lotuses. Once, while driving across New Hampshire, I came across a small foreign repair shop with an MGA and a Bugeye Sprite in the front drive. I stopped to look and inside was a British Racing Green Lotus Seven. I felt dizzy. I knew the fates were being kind. It was worn and faded and a thing of beauty. But, as a poor college student, there was no way for me to afford it. I had to leave my dream parked on someone else's garage floor. That car haunted me for a long time.

A few years later I was a productive member of society and working as an engineer in South Carolina. Early one Sunday morning, upon opening to the automotive classifieds as was my custom, I saw an ad. It was for a 1964 Lotus Seven. I couldn't believe my eyes. I stared at the ad for a few long seconds before diving to the phone. The car was two towns away, about 50 miles. It didn't matter. I got the directions and fired up my 1965 Austin Healey 3000, the only thing I had to barter with to get my long-sought Lotus.

I don't remember anything of the drive, my visions of what I would find blurring my eyesight. I found the place right away, a U-rent-it storage building just outside of Anderson, South Carolina. I knew from the long envious look the Lotus owner gave my sparkling blue and silver Healey that I had brought the right bargaining tool. He slid open the garage door and there sat the object of my fifteen year search.

Frankly, it didn't look that good, especially next to the sleek sports car I had brought to the party. But under that film of dust sat two huge Weber carburetors and the finned alloy valve cover of a special Cosworth cylinder head. It was a 1500cc Ford Cosworth powered missile, the most potent version of the Lotus Super Seven of the mid-sixties. It was British Racing Green with a yellow nose, just like the Lotus *The Prisoner* drove in that sixties British television thriller. The original fiberglass fenders were shabby, but new rear ones came with the car and the front ones could be saved. It wasn't running, but the owner claimed the engine had been recently rebuilt. Gleaming blue paint on the engine indicated it had at least been recently out of the chassis.

We traded even; my big beautiful Healey for this sorry pile of steel tubes, aluminum panels and shredded fiberglass fenders. He threw in delivery. I think he felt sorry for me. I learned a lot about tube frame cars in the next few months. I bought a MIG-welder and replaced cracked tubes and added bracing for the engine and transmission. I stripped the paint off the main tub, leaving it in polished aluminum, and painted the hood, cowl and fenders their original green. The nose I painted arctic white. The combination was quite attractive. It took a while to get the engine running and with those large Webers, it never liked to idle or drive slowly. But once it was all sorted out, the Lotus was scary fast. I took it to a bunch of local autocrosses and was beaten only by formula cars and once by a Lotus Europa on racing slicks. Just as in my dreams, it was fast and fun and made me want to laugh out loud each time I drove it.

I got a call a few months ago from one of my college roommates, wanting to know if I wanted to buy my old Lotus back. Suddenly, I was fifteen again, feeling all the lust I had felt all those years ago. He had purchased the car from me when I had decided that racing a Mini Cooper on the track would be more fun than driving a Super Seven on the street. He had kept the Lotus as original as possible, making only subtle improvements and resisting the temptation to heavily modify it. He wanted it to go to someone who would understand that philosophy. For a week I agonized over my lost love. Finally, I called him and told him I just couldn't do it. Too many other cars had come and gone. Too many others had worked their way into my heart. I had a garage full of them and dreams of others I wanted to own. I had already been in love with my old Lotus. I had moved on to cars more like Isabella Rosalini and less like Alicia Silverstone. I wouldn't fall into the same trap so many classic car collectors had. I wouldn't try to recapture my youth. After all, you are only allowed to be fifteen once.

CHAPTER 20

Happy Trail(er)s:
Sooner or later, you've got to tow

If you mess around with cars long enough, the day will come when you will have to haul a car on a trailer. Old cars breakdown, racing cars need to get to the track, once-in-a-lifetime project car deals materialize or sometimes you just need to move more than one car from point A to point B. Trailering a car can be tricky, but the good news is the more you do it, the easier it becomes.

One of the first things to decide is whether or not you need to own a trailer. If you only tow a car once or twice a year, you probably can get by renting a car-hauler trailer from one of the national rental companies. These are easy to use and most even have an extra insurance policy available to cover possible damages to the vehicle on the trailer. Insurance companies are a bit strange on towing but most provide coverage based upon the tow vehicle. Still, that is a good thing to check before heading out on the highway. There are some limitations that rental companies apply to what vehicles can be used for towing. Don't expect to show up with your VW Jetta and come home with a trailer. Pickup trucks and sport utility vehicles are preferred. Rental car trailers can carry fairly large cars and have integrated strap systems to keep the car in place.

If you have a racing car or want to trailer a fragile car to shows, it makes sense to own your own trailer. Except you aren't just looking for a trailer. You also have to consider what vehicle you will tow with. There are a lot of things to consider but, not surprisingly, the type of cars you will be towing makes a very good starting point. The trailer and tow vehicle requirements for my lightweight vintage Formula Vee are a lot different than those for my much heavier Jaguar XK150. If you own a 1950's American car, you will need a huge trailer and powerful tow vehicle just to move the thing out of the driveway.

There is a progression of rationalization that often occurs when it comes to trailers. When I started vintage racing my MG Midget, I had an older Jeep Cherokee and decided a lightweight trailer would work just fine. I bought a tilt-bed single axle trailer and the combination was great. I could tow up to 70-mph without problems and the Jeep wasn't straining on trips to vintage races around the Midwest. I liked the trailer because it didn't need ramps and was easy to push around when it was empty.

My next racer was an MG TD. This car is slightly larger than the 60's Midget and just fit onto the trailer. But, when I began to tow at speed, the weight distribution on the trailer was all wrong. At anything above 55-mph, a vicious sway would set in, threatening to upset the entire rig. This kind of sway occurs suddenly and is very difficult to control. The tow vehicle is forced from side to side, like the tail wagging the dog. The only remedy is to slow down until the motion stops, usually at a much lower speed than it started. Using the tow vehicle brakes to control this sway can actually make it worse, although some success can be attained using just the trailer brakes. It is very scary. I tried taking the spare wheel off the back of the MG and placing weight on the front of the trailer to get more tongue weight on the hitch, but it was always a marginal setup and I finally sold the single axle trailer before it killed me.

I knew I would need a double axle trailer to carry the MG TD, but I also wanted to keep my 6-cylinder Jeep to tow it. I finally went to a trailer builder and had a special, shortened trailer built with a fourteen-foot long bed instead of the more usual sixteen-foot version. The bed is wooden, which is heavy, but the full floor means I can carry a variety of different cars with different widths without worry. The shorter length makes the trailer lighter and easier to maneuver. The trailer has electric brakes on one axle and I supplied four new high-quality radial tires for its wheels. The MG TD fits on with space to spare and towing on the flat and level at 70-mph isn't a problem for my Jeep.

The double axle trailer does have some drawbacks. It is too heavy to easily move around by hand. The bed doesn't tilt, so I need to carry ramps, which stow under the trailer but rattle. On the plus side, it can carry cars up to the size of my Jaguar coupe and as small as my Formula Vee and is easy to store behind the house and out of view of the neighbors. This might have been the best possible long-term trailer solution.

Then we moved to the mountains of Virginia. Suddenly, my old Jeep Cherokee, which had no problems maintaining 70-mph on the flat highways of the Midwest, struggled to keep 45-mph on the long grades of the Blue Ridge Mountains. The onset of transmission problems in the Jeep were probably brought on by the added strain of towing up and over the hills and ridges. The answer was simple. I needed a more powerful tow vehicle. A used Chevrolet or GMC Suburban with a hearty V-8 engine seemed like a good choice.

Living in the country as I did, I now had space enough to easily store an enclosed trailer. There are advantages to enclosed trailers, especially on rainy days at the racetrack where they can act as a dry and comfy summer cottage. Security on the road is another factor, plus the luxury of storing the car, its parts and tools in the trailer between races. Because I was buying a stronger tow vehicle, I could get one that would pull an enclosed trailer. See what I mean about a progression?

Another concern when towing a car is how to attach it to the trailer. My preference is ratcheting cargo straps. The 9,000 pound versions work well and four of them provide plenty of excess capacity for a 2,000 pound racing car. It is important to find something sturdy on the car to attach the hooks to; an axle or frame member is a good choice. Make sure, however, that the straps aren't caught on a sharp edge that could cause cutting as the load moves over bumps in the road. Extra axle straps are available to protect the tie-downs from grease and oil and to make the job easier. I like to place at least one strap through a frame member to snug the vehicle's springs down and keep its suspension from moving around too much. I prefer the trailer springs to do the work over bumps. My trailer has welded-in rings to attach the straps, to help ensure a secure tie-down. Some racers put an electric winch at the front of their trailers to help load a disabled car and this cable can also be used to tie down a vehicle.

When trailering, it is important to remember that the extra load will dramatically increase stopping distances and make acceleration to merge onto a freeway more demanding. The braking system on your tow vehicle must be in top condition and most trailers have electric brakes or surge brakes to help provide more stopping power. Electric brakes have a controller inside the vehicle that you can adjust to compensate for the load you are carrying on the trailer. It is important to read the instructions and set the brakes properly to avoid premature trailer wheel locking. For really heavy loads, special four-bar trailer hitches are available that help with trailer stability and to maintain control.

There is a special kind of magic that towing a vintage car on a trailer can bring: First, early in the pre-dawn morning, heading to a far-off racetrack, full of hope and excitement for the upcoming weekend. And then, heading for home late at night, after a successful race, with the faint odor of racing fuel in the air and adrenaline still coursing your veins. A quick glance in the mirror confirms the glow of the taillights against the MG's upright grille and headlights.

Several years ago I attended a vintage race at Silverstone in England. At the back of the paddock were a bunch of rickety single axle trailers being towed by beat-up old vans and saloon cars. On the trailers were D-type Jaguars, Lister Chevrolets and a whole host of exotic sports racing cars. At U.S. vintage races, it isn't unusual to see a 40-foot long tractor trailer rig carrying a Bugeye Sprite. Ours is a country of big distances and even bigger egos. I may yet get an enclosed trailer, but there is some romance to towing a vintage car to a vintage race on an open trailer. Every gas stop is a chance to talk about your pride and joy. On the highway, kids wave, women smile and men give a thumbs up as they share for a moment the unique kind of pleasures that old cars bring.

CHAPTER 21

Tribal Customs:
Buy a car, make new friends

In the early days of the sports car movement, owners would frequently wave to one another as they passed. As in most things in life, there was a definite protocol to such displays of good will and sportsmanship. Drivers of cars on the upper end of the evolutionary scale, marques that had won at LeMans, like Ferrari, Jaguar and Porsche, would rarely initiate a wave, but occasionally lower themselves enough to politely return one. MG owners would wave at anyone, but most especially at other MG owners, no doubt in congratulations that the other driver actually managed to keep their car running long enough to drive it. Sports car and, actually, European car ownership, made you a member of a different group, a breed apart from the dullards who drove more ordinary Detroit iron.

Buying a brand-new European car today still brings with it a certain feeling of taste and refinement, but some of that feeling of bonhomie toward fellow Europhiles has been lost. Hardly anybody ever waves anymore. The exception is owners of older sports cars and sedans from England and the continent. When two of these old-timers pass on the highway, their owners usually raise a hand in a gesture of appreciation. In a way, it's a form of the old secret handshake. Driving an old car, especially an old sports car, still sets you apart from the madding crowd. More importantly, it makes you a member of a different tribe, one with its own customs, rituals and protocols.

One of the first things you notice after buying an old sports car is that it needs a lot more maintenance and upkeep than does a modern Blastomobile. If you are lucky, your old car came with a shop manual that tells you how to do many of these things. If not, you need to find out more about your new toy. A trip to the bookstore is a good first step. The automotive sections of most big chain stores are filled with history and how-to books for most of the old cars we know and love. Even the fairly arcane is reasonably well-served today. After checking out the book selections, head over to the magazine racks. *European Car* and a variety of magazines from overseas cater to sports car owners and you will eventually need the advertising inside to help you find parts and more information.

At some point in your old car ownership a reading knowledge just won't be enough. When a seemingly irreplaceable part breaks, or you need more information than the books and manuals can give you, you will need to talk to somebody who knows the cars and where to find the parts. Maybe you start at the local auto parts store or repair shop, casually mentioning you have an unusual car and need to find someone who knows about it. If you are lucky, a club exists for like-minded owners of the marque and one of the members can point you in the right directions. Eventually, someone will know someone who will be able to send you to another person who has what you need. It is truly amazing what is out there if you have the patience to look for it. There are people who know more about your car than the people who built it, and who have special parts and accessories the factory forgot it ever produced.

When I bought my first Austin Healey 3000, I drove it home wondering why the clutch seemed to slip so badly. When I put the car in my garage and drained the oil from the overdrive, it was filled with shards of metal. I pulled the overdrive unit off and found the inside looked like a grenade had exploded inside of it. As I was driving the car on a shoestring budget, this was a major tragedy. A rebuilt Laycock de Normanville overdrive for my Healey cost several hundred dollars; much more than I could afford. I put the word out with my sports car owning friends and at the local foreign auto parts store. One person led to another and I was finally directed to a boarded up garage a couple of towns away. I met the owner early one evening and gave him $50 for a grease-covered object that he claimed was an overdrive unit for a big Healey. The strange part of the deal is that I also had to buy the spare front and rear bumpers he had for a Healey 3000 for another $25. How could I refuse?

The rarer a car is, the more critical it becomes to get tied into the right network. If you have an MG, Triumph or Jaguar, finding parts is easy. Just call Moss Motors and they can supply just about every part you need. You could literally build up a complete car from their catalogs. Owners of Porsches are extremely well served by a variety of specialists, but if you want something a bit different, say, for an old Volvo or Lotus or Hillman, then the search becomes a bit more difficult. You have to get to know the right people and, often, to get that rare bracket or special factory part, you must succumb to owning a parts car. In the past, almost any foreign car that wasn't running could be a parted out. Today, the values of such old hulks are much higher, and "parts cars" have become "restorable" which makes finding a true parts car pretty hopeless.

Racing old cars brings the whole process of meeting other members of the tribe into much sharper focus. The stress of competition puts a lot more strain on the cars, and parts simply wear out that much quicker. Fine if you are racing the same car as everyone else. Not so good if your car is a one of a kind or the last of its breed.

My friend Marvin Primack races a very rare Ausper T-3 Formula Junior. Ausper built racing cars between 1960 and 1962 in England. Marv's car is absolutely beautiful to look at and he drives it with great verve. One year, while racing at Mid-Ohio, he was tapped from behind by another car. He came straight in to check for damage and found the right rear suspension upright had cracked. "It's the only irreplaceable piece on the whole car," reports Marv. The upright on the Ausper is made from Elektron, an aluminum-magnesium alloy from the early sixties. Marv disassembled the suspension, removed the part, and went in search of a welder. The track maintenance chief couldn't weld the piece but sent Marv across town to his cousin. The cousin took one look at the part and admitted that he didn't have the correct tools to weld aluminum alloys, but his pal Rick could do it. Marv got instructions to Rick's place in the next town. Rick could do the job, but didn't have the right welding rod for magnesium. He began to give Marv directions to his friend Kenny's house and suddenly said, "You won't find it will you? Get in my truck and I'll take you there..."

Upon arriving, Marv found that Kenny had a shop behind his house filled with tools and devices he had built from scratch. Kenny took the part in his weld-scarred hands, nodded and began grinding a deep trough into the cracked suspension piece. After a while he took out his welder and began to weld. He would weld for about five minutes and then sit back and talk for about ten minutes. Marv calculated if he could just hurry Kenny along, he could still make the last race at the end of the day. Marv looked at his watch pointedly while Kenny welded a bit and talked a lot. Finally, Kenny said, "You notice how slow I am going on this job? That's because the hub bearings are still in your suspension piece and if I weld too quickly they will get overheated and ruined." Marv stopped looking at his watch. When Kenny was all finished, Marv asked how much the job would be. Kenny squinted at him a moment and then said "fifteen should cover it..."

Marv Primack's experience isn't at all an isolated case. Almost anyone who races an old car has a similar story. Most times the people who are the most help, who are willing to open their repair shop after hours or drive miles out of their way, don't even own an old sports car or vintage racer. They just see an opportunity to use their abilities and resources to help another person out of a jam. In a sense they are members of their own tribe. Sports car owners may not wave at each other as much as they used to but, in a sense, the tribal customs have become much stronger. As Marv Primack, an orthopedic surgeon who does almost all his own work on his cars explains, "I would never have a chance to meet people like Rick and Kenny if I wasn't racing my Ausper."

CHAPTER 22

Pack Rat Fever:
Moving the parts that move you

I got an e-mail from Fred Sisson. Fred lived in Atlanta but was in the process of moving to Indiana. Fred is a Morgan sports car guru. He literally wrote the book on the care and feeding of these charismatic British roadsters. He races an F-Series Morgan trike with great élan and is a founding member of the Southeastern Vintage Sports Car Racing and Grit Tasting Society. Fred's e-mail was lamenting the whole process of packing and moving, especially for someone who has been in their house for more than a decade, collecting a yard full of cars and filling a garage and basement with old, broken and obsolete parts that seem impossible to throw away. He closed his note wondering why he was so carefully packing frayed speedometer cables, cracked distributor caps and broken rear axle parts for cars he didn't even own anymore. Being in the middle of a move myself, I could instantly relate. I too, am a pack rat.

I've said it before. In the days before nearly instantaneous delivery replacement parts from people like Moss Motors, Victoria British and The Roadster Factory, if you wanted to own an old foreign car, you had to be a pack rat. The term seems to have negative connotations to some, but salting away for future use an old but usable bit of British hardware was often the only way to keep an old sports car on the road. Throwing a greasy lump of metal into an old cardboard box and storing it under the workbench could be looked at as a sort of insurance policy against future breakdowns. Some (not me of course) would even claim that keeping old spare parts would keep the ones still on the car from breaking. The downside to this superstition is that it would almost guarantee that the next part to break on your beloved old crock would be one for which you didn't have a replacement in a box under the workbench.

Let's examine this a bit closer. Speedometer cables in old British sports cars are notoriously unreliable. One minute you are zipping down the highway with the needle bouncing around in the vicinity of 65-mph, and the next the needle is motionless at the bottom of the scale. This is because the British made their speedometer cables from vermicelli that they received from the Italians as reparations after the war. In the old days, you would probably end up driving without a speedometer for months or even years. It could be that long before you were able to find a replacement cable in a junkyard or automotive flea market. Having done so and, therefore, realizing just how valuable and rare speedometer cables for your car were, you would be reticent to throw the old one away. Once it's coiled up, the thing takes up very little space and by pounding a nail into a wall you could hang it up where the car would see it in the garage, granting you immunity from any similar future failures. Now, of course, it is much easier to get speedometer cables for most cars, but the genetic code of the automotive pack rat makes us repeat the redundant behavior.

It isn't just speedometer cables that engender such a response among car enthusiasts. Frayed throttle cables, cracked distributor caps, worn points and condensers, old spark plugs, u-joints for driveshafts, tie rod ends with just a bit of play in them, leaky water pumps, streaky wiper blades and stretched fan belts clutter our garage floor space, quietly working their mojo to prevent future failures on the objects of our affections. But beyond this there is the constant, albeit forlorn, hope that if something were to suddenly break, we would have a slightly worn part that we could plug into the car and keep it on the road. Even if we no longer own a particular vehicle, in the back of our minds the MacGyver in us makes us believe it would be possible to adapt that MGB water pump to fit an Audi Coupe.

Garages can absorb an amazing amount of stuff and after a while the boxes and cans and cartons of used and abused parts become a part of the scenery, adding their own visual complexity and aromatic karma to the essence of the workshop. In time you forget what parts are even there. They can peacefully coexist for years, undisturbed, as they attain a quiet dignity and a coating of dust. Until, that is, it comes time to move.

Any ordinary, rational person would look at moving as a perfect chance to throw away this accumulation of worn-out and useless parts in the garage. It's a sort of fresh start that bright-eyed zealots are always trying to make. But what about sentimentality? Sure, I don't own a Bugeye Sprite anymore, but I really liked that car so shouldn't I save a pair of slightly discolored front turn signal lenses in case I ever own another one? And what about that pair of MGB SU carburetors? I replaced them with a Weber and the car ran great, but who knows if I might have a need for a good pair of SUs some day? Besides, with some cutting of the manifold, they might fit on another car. You immediately begin to see the problem. No part is too obscure and, in fact, the more obscure the better. That's why I have such goodies as a rear brake rebuild kit for a Morgan Plus Four that I no longer own, a full upper and lower gasket set for a six-cylinder Mercedes-Benz engine, a triple-carb setup for a Saab sports racer, five brand-new steel wheels for a Porsche 914 (don't ask), a dome light for an Alfa Romeo Guilia and the aforementioned MGB carburetors. See? It's the pack rat's genetic code.

If the move is a short one and the distances aren't too great, much of the detritus of the garage can be quietly and surreptitiously transferred from one location to the other, a few boxes at a time. If you take just a few things at a time it won't seem like so much stuff. The problem isn't getting them out of the old place, it's finding a spot to stash them in the new place. Putting them out in plain view is an invitation to their disposal as friends and loved ones wonder openly why anyone would want to move the broken overdrive unit for an Austin Healey 3000. I suggest you casually look for places the parts can go as soon as possible in the home buying process. Certainly by the final walk-through inspection you should have a plan in mind where those BMW 2002 front struts are going to hide. Then, each time you go from the old place to the new, you can carry a few more talismans of automotive good fortune with you.

Long distance moves pose bigger problems. When I moved from Virginia to Ohio a couple years ago, I managed to fill an entire trash dumpster with bits and pieces I had been collecting for years. As soon as you throw something away, you naturally then have an immediate and pressing need for it and I spent several months after arriving in my new shop looking for things that were now part of a Virginia landfill. More importantly, I lost a significant amount of good automotive karma that I am just now starting to get back.

Perhaps the hardest things to part with are magazines and repair manuals. I have boxes and bookshelves of them. The manuals can be found at almost any used bookstore. Generally, when I sell an old car to someone, I give them the repair manuals I have for the car. Yet somehow I seem to still have a wide range of manuals for cars like the Saab 99 and the Ford Fiesta. It isn't just cars that I have owned, others seem to have crept into my collection. I will probably never own a Renault Dauphine, nor do I want one, but at least I have the satisfaction of knowing I have a repair manual for one should the unthinkable occur. Car magazines are even worse, because whenever I start to pack or unpack them I get completely preoccupied reading and the job always takes much longer than I thought it would.

There is another answer of course. You can transfer the beneficial aura that comes from your used and worn-out parts, manuals and classic car magazines to another eager enthusiast. There are several ways to do this, but the most time-honored way is to load them all into a rented trailer and bring them to a collector car flea market. This is sort of the ultimate pack-rat experience as vendors position piles of worn-out and useless parts on tables. It is said you can make money doing this but the problem is that often a truly dedicated automotive pack-rat will return with a trailer filled with a different set of parts and books than they arrived with. In the process of selling your stuff, you gain the where-with-all to get even more. If this seems counter-productive you will understand why I no longer go to flea-markets. Still, there are those who claim that they can get rid of their used up bits and pieces and feel good about passing them on to someone with empty garage space.

None of this would help Fred of course, not that he was looking for help or advice anyway. I suspect his move will involve more than a few trips between Georgia and Indiana and that more than a few of the parts that he moves will be for cars he doesn't even own any longer. He will save them because they are cool or rare or difficult to find, not because he needs them. For me, that will be a good thing. Fred is a pack rat in the best sense of the word and when I can't find something in my own modest piles of parts under my workbench, I'll know just who to call.

CHAPTER 23

True Confessions:
I am an Internet junkie

They say the first step to curing an addiction is to admit you have a problem. Okay, here it is: My name is Kevin and I am an Internet automotive auction junkie. There, that wasn't so hard. Now can I go back to cruising through eBay to find the cars of my dreams?

Consider this. Just today, while looking in the Collector Car section of eBay, I found a 1974 Iso Lele in Minneapolis, formerly the 1974 New York Auto Show display car, for $10,202. Or how about a 1963 Chajka Limousine, a personal gift from Soviet President Brezhnev to some Russian official, for under $10,000. Okay, so the car is still in the former Soviet Union, how hard could it be to get it out? Of course these are some of the really exotic examples. Most of the collector cars listed for auction are good old American iron: Mustangs, Camaros and Chevelles, Corvettes, Plymouths and Cadillacs seem the most common. Yet a surprising number are European cars, and many of these are downright desirable.

Here is a 1958 Morgan Plus-Four Drophead for a reasonable $18,000. And another bargain, a 1955 Austin Healey 100-4 offered at $8600 on Long Island. There are an abundance of early 1970's BMW 2002's, all in the $3,500 to $7,000 range. VW Beetles remain a refreshing mainstay of the foreign collector car market, prices in the $2500 to $6,000 range. A 1974 Mercedes-Benz 280C Coupe in Kansas seems cheap at $1500 as does a 1959 Porsche 356 Coupe for $12,000 in Des Moines.

Porsche 356's are high on my list of desirable sports cars and there always seem to be a fair number of them on the online auctions in the $8,000 to $15,000 range. Contrast this to the $20-$30,000 they seem to bring from classic car dealers and clearly something is missing here. The problem is readily apparent: You are buying the car sight unseen. This may be fine for a late model car, with modern rust proofing and foolproof mechanical components, but how smart is it trusting a few grainy digital images and a seller's description of a thirty-year-old sports car?

The Porsche 356 is a good example. Anyone who has ever owned one, or people who sell them for a living, will tell you that condition is all important. These early Porsches have a bad habit of rusting. Rusting a lot. Even on the Coupes the floors and fenders can be barely attached to the car through a lacework of corroded metal. Colanders can have more solidity. In fact, rusting is so common on these cars that replacing the floors on an otherwise sound car is considered a normal part of keeping it on the road and, if done well, isn't a reason to reject a car that you want to drive. The other thing that determines the value of a 356 is its originality. The engines on these air-cooled beauties had a lot in common with air-cooled VW engines, so it was not uncommon to replace the Porsche unit with a Volkswagen one when engine problems occurred. There are ways to protect yourself reguarding this possibility. You could have a qualified Porsche 356 expert look at your intended purchase before you bid but, remember, most of the cars are being offered by private individuals and the chances of arranging the viewing in the week or two that the auction is open could be next to impossible.

Even if the deals sometimes seem too good to be true, it doesn't keep the act of browsing from being entertaining, especially if you know something about the models of cars that are offered. Not to pick on Porsches, but here is a 1972 Porsche 914 in Pennsylvania for $660. The ad says the car "needs some work" and goes on to say that the work needed is rust repair. I have owned a couple of these much maligned mid-engine oddities, and have seen even more of them in auto parts junkyards. What the ravages of rust can do to a 914 has to be seen to be believed. I have seen whole cars, otherwise unmarked from collision, broken in half simply from corrosion. How bad would a $660 car from Pennsylvania be, purchased sight unseen? Another ad for a 1962 Jaguar Mark II 3.8 Sedan brings 17 bids. The car is in San Jose, California and bidding seems to have stalled in the $2,650 range. I look at the online photograph of the car and it looks pretty crusty around the edges with corrosion. How much money could a person spend on a Jaguar Mark II sedan in crusty shape making it street worthy? Wouldn't it be easier and possibly cheaper to buy a new XK8?

And yet, like gawkers who drive past an accident and are unable to keep from looking, I can't turn my eyes away from my computer screen. Each morning, at the crack of dawn, I am on eBay's Collector Car Auction, checking what deals will end that day, dreaming about the possibilities. When I first started checking the auctions daily, I would only look at what was new. I would savor the entire week, pondering the joys of owning a Humber Super Snipe or Matra Djet, as I watched others drive the prices higher and higher with their bidding. Lately though, as my addiction has grown more acute, I have begun to crave the instant satisfaction of seeing a car for the first time on the last day of its auction. The drama is higher as the hours tick down to the final moments when a surprise bidder can pop in and steal the car away. Clearly, this is how the real players play the game. Sometimes, a poor orphan of a car will lack any bids until the last few minutes when, mercifully, a bid will finally be offered. More often than not these are coming from dealers who must believe they will be able to resell the same car for a profit.

After watching for so long, I finally decided I should try to be a part of the game. I had already bid on a few car parts and books, even winning a couple of auctions for parts that will eventually find their way onto my pre-war sprint car. But I wanted to bid on a whole car, just like the big boys. My wife and I have always wanted a Mini to drive around the city. I used to race one of these little shoeboxes and there is nothing quite like one for pure driving fun. I kept my eye on the eBay auctions and finally found a 1973 Mini 1275 GT located in Florida. The bidding on this car had stalled with the 18th bid at $4,600, which was below the reserve the seller had placed on the car. This reserve price is kept secret and if the final bidding is below reserve, the seller has no obligation to sell the car. The car I was interested in was dark blue with a white top and cute Minilight alloy wheels. The interior looked fine and the car appeared rust-free, at least from its photos. It was now or never and this tiny, charismatic car seemed to be a good place to start. For two days I watched the auction. The final day arrived.

I waited patiently that day, checking on eBay every few hours to see if the price had changed. There were no other bidders and the price was firmly planted at $4,600. I waited during the last hour, expecting to see the bid change. Finally, with five minutes left, I jumped in with a bid of $4,800, a bargain for a 1970s Mini. With one minute to go, my name flashed onto the screen as the high bidder, but still below the reserve price. My heart soared with the thrill of competition. This was like racing and I was in the lead! The next time the screen flashed, it noted that the auction had ended. I looked at the price, it was now $5,000 and the reserve had been met. I looked at the buyer and it wasn't me. In the last thirty seconds, a craftier buyer had placed a bid that surpassed mine and topped the secret reserve price as well. They had won and I had finished second. In an auction, that meant that I had lost. I didn't really need the Mini. But it sure looked like a good one and if it's even close to being as good as it looks, somebody got it for a great price.

It doesn't matter, of course. The fun in all of this is in the hunt. Prehistoric man was by nature a hunter, beating the bushes and stalking his prey with stealth and cunning. Those who were less cunning than the others went without, until they learned the wiles of the game. The more you hunted, the better you became. As much as we may wish to resist it, the primitive urges are still too strong. Every morning you can find me on the Internet prairie stalking my prey, sifting through the possibilities, always ready to pounce. Best of all, in the last few days, a new hunting ground has suddenly opened before me, one where the game is even more plentiful.

I have just discovered that eBay also auctions motorcycles.

CHAPTER 24
Another Golden Age

If you love cars, especially European cars, your time has come. After losing their way and all but abandoning the US market to the Japanese in the late eighties, European manufacturers like Mercedes-Benz, Audi, BMW, Jaguar, Porsche, Saab, Volvo and Volkswagen have come charging back with a vengeance. We were told the roadster market is dead. Enter the SLK, Z3 and the Boxster. We were told nobody wants sedans anymore. Enter the Saab 9-5, Volvo S70, Audi A6 and VW Passat. High-end sports cars? The new Porsche 911, the Jaguar XK8 and the Ferrari Maranello are the best those companies have ever produced. Even the sport utility market is under pressure from Land Rover, Mercedes and BMW. European cars are back on the lists of car buyers and we are entering another gilded age for Eurocentric car enthusiasts.

But as glittering as the new line-up of stars may be, there is a group of aging actors from a previous golden age that should be grabbing some of your attention. There has never been a better time to own and old European car. They have style, they have class and they practically ooze charm and character, and, sometimes, a little oil. It doesn't even have to be a traditional string-backed glove sports car from the early fifties. The Europeans built a bunch of cars in the sixties and seventies that are fun, if not fast and interesting, if not overly refined. Best of all, unless you choose something completely outrageous, they can be purchased for tens of thousands less than their 1998 counter-parts.

Do you like sports cars? For under ten thousand dollars you could have an MGB or Midget, a Triumph TR6, TR7 or Spitfire, a Fiat 124 or X1/9 or a Porsche 912 or 914. Have a bit more to spend? How about a fifteen to twenty year old Porsche 911? I've driven the new Boxster on some of the best roads in the country. It's fast and comfortable and razor-sharp, everything a sports car should be. I've also owned a 1973 Porsche 911. Comfortable? Not like the Boxster, but not bad. Quiet? Not really, not with that busy six-cylinder engine stuffed into the tail. Fast? Yes, in its time it was among the fastest. Today there are hot coupes that are quicker, but an old 911 has a charm that even the new Boxster cannot approach. Its lines and forms are simple and purposeful and it doesn't carry all of the gold-chain baggage that later 911's were forced to haul. A nice, clean 911 will cost you about a quarter of the price of a new Boxster.

The ultimate sports car for most people is a Ferrari. A new Maranello with all the trimmings will cost you $204,000. It's a great car in the grand tradition of Ferraris gone by. But a 308 Ferrari is also a great car, albeit one with only eight instead of twelve cylinders. But a mid-1970s Ferrari 308 is now as cheap as Ferrari ownership has ever been. Figure $25-$30,000 for a reasonably well-kept example. Sure, service will be expensive and you will probably get to know a mechanic named Mario, but it is a true, red-blooded Ferrari. How could you refuse?

But let's get our feet back on the ground. A good, usable BMW 2002 can be purchased for under $5,000. These were the cars that put BMW into the game and they are every bit the definition of the expression "ultimate driving machine." Their replacement, the BMW 320I, is a pretty good car, too, and suffers only in comparison to the original. Not what you had in mind? How about a Volvo 142E? This

2-door quick brick came with fuel injection and an attitude quite unlike the usually staid Swedes. It was a spiritual successor to the Volvo 123GT factory racers from the late-sixties and is almost as much fun as the BMW on a twisty road. Strong and tough, quite a few have survived, though most are in pretty rough shape as the virtues of this boxy car are just now beginning to be appreciated. If you want the same sort of car, but live in snow country, how about a Saab? The 99EMS from the mid-seventies has front-wheel drive and was designed to go head to head with the BMW 2002. Later, the Saab 900 Turbo was quick and comfortable and a good one will cost less than $5,000.

Let's say you want a luxury car. How about a mid-seventies Mercedes sedan, a Jaguar XJ6 or even a Rolls Royce? Be careful though, these cars are all very complicated and very expensive to repair. Still, showing up at the country club behind the formidable grille of your Rolls-Royce Silver Shadow, for less than half the cost of a Lexus, must be somewhat satisfying.

I have been driving old cars for the better part of two decades. Usually European, frequently British. Yes, they are less reliable than modern cars. True, not every repair shop wants to work on them. The secret to making them reliable is to replace worn and suspect parts before they begin to cause you a problem. This can mean having the starter and alternator or generator rebuilt before the car refuses to start or the battery is dead. It is also true that my old cars are not my primary means of transportation, which means that I always have a backup plan and another way to get to the places I need to go. On the other hand, I always seem to have more fun going mundane places than people who drive their modern hermetically-sealed transport module. The bark of a small displacement high-compression engine, the rush of wind around a vertical flat-pained windshield or the deep-throated burble of a long-stroke six-cylinder engine easily competes with anything you would care to play on your mega-watt in-car stereo.

For a long time, if you owned an old European car you also probably owned one or two parts cars and knew of at least two or three other derelicts to scavenge components from. Thankfully, for most cars, those times have changed. Instead of pulling worn-out old bits off of rusting hulks to replace your broken parts, you can now use the phone and order almost anything you need. British sports car owners are well served by companies like Moss Motors who manufacture replacement parts to the same specifications as the originals. Other companies cater to old BMW, Porsche, Volvo, Saab, Fiat and Mercedes models and can provide almost everything to keep an old car on the road.

What about safety and legal requirements? It's true that these older cars don't have air bags and anti-lock brakes. But European manufacturers were generally at the front of safety in the sixties and seventies and most of their cars have well-designed three point seat belts and occupant protecting crush zones. If you religiously wear your belts, an air bag only decreases your chance of injury by a few percent, so safety in an older car largely comes down to you. Just be sure to inspect your seatbelts for wear and fraying and replace them if you have any doubts. Many of these older cars were sold at the beginnings of exhaust emission control and their systems have probably been circumvented to improve drivability. Some states, notably California, used to require that all the emissions hardware be in place, regardless of how ineffectual it really was. Recently that requirement has changed. Ironically, most older cars can pass a state tail-pipe test if they are kept well-tuned and adjusted, which is also the key to reliability.

If I have convinced you that there is an old European car in your future, the fun part is about to start. Finding old cars is pretty easy.

Look in your local newspaper or classified advertising magazine. You will find literally hundreds of older cars that are just waiting for you to take them home. Take your time, however, shop carefully. Avoid cars with too much rust and, if you have your doubts, bring your find to a trusted mechanic for a check over. Spending a bit more for a better car is always better than buying cheap and then having lots of work to do. Scan the classifieds every day and act promptly when you see something. Others are out there doing the same thing and competition for good cars is pretty strong. And be patient. Eventually you will pull into a driveway and there will be the car of your dreams. A car that has charm and warmth and stirs your blood. A car you will cherish and enjoy. A car from another golden age.

CHAPTER 25

The Ones That Got Away

Whenever car guys get together (guys is non-gender specific for you politically correct-types. I know lots of women who are car guys), one topic that eventually surfaces is the great cars that got away. Anyone who likes old cars has a story. Sometimes more than one. Usually it is a story of being at the "right place at the wrong time." Or the familiar "day late and dollar short." Everyone has heard the one about the Ferrari or perhaps Mercedes-Benz 300SL, left in a barn by a son who went to war and never came home. But it doesn't even really have to be a great car to be a great story. Anything from the 1950s or 60s that is unusual and European (is that an oxymoron?) will usually suffice. Extra points are given for sports cars.

In my own case, I have several such stories. I grew up in St. Petersburg, Florida in the late 1960s. Back then it was a sleepy retirement community. It also had a few aerospace companies filled with engineers whose main preoccupation was sending astronauts to the moon and back. I think this concentration of engineering-types is the reason that sports cars were plentiful. Nothing like a twin-cam Alfa engine or a Porsche transaxle to keep an engineer happy on the off-hours. Add in a few tweed-jacketed MG driving professors from a couple of local liberal arts colleges, and it made for a foreign-car-rich environment.

I used to prowl the back rows of used car lots. That's where the weird and unusual could be found. That's where the bargains were. In those days, almost every used car lot in St. Petersburg had at least one Alfa Romeo, either a coupe or a spider, invariably ratty but complete. The asking price was always $400. I wonder who set those prices? It didn't matter what part of the city you went to, the price for a back row Alfa was $400.

There was a car lot not far from my house. I rode my bike there every day after school. The attraction was three lovely MGA roadsters. At least they were lovely in my eyes. Two of them had their engines out and apart in their trunks. None of them had tops or even much left of the interiors. But they had that smell. That moldy, British-car-gone-to-seed mixed with stale gasoline and brake fluid odor that I would later come to know so well. I begged my parents to come and talk to the proprietor about buying them. One day I rode up on my faithful three-speed and they were gone. I screwed up my courage and asked the owner where they went. "I sent them to the crusher, they gave me $100 bucks for all three..." Three MGAs weren't the only things that got crushed that day.

MG's are a recurring theme in my life. On another car lot, next to the Porsche dealer, there sat the prettiest car I had ever seen. It was light yellow with a black top and side curtains. It was an MG TD with Iowa license plates. I rode my bicycle past that car a hundred times. I didn't mind the small dent in the right rear fender. It made it look more approachable. Finally, I pleaded with my parents and they asked the price. It was $1200. More than I could afford. More than they could afford. Twenty-five years later I bought a light yellow MG TD in St. Petersburg and brought it back to Michigan. I have always wondered if my car had waited for me for all those years.

My parents weren't insensitive to my serious case of sports car lust. My dad came home from work one day and told me he had seen a really small sports car a few miles away. He thought it might be a Bugeye Sprite, but it looked smaller and had a badge with a "B" on the hood. I knew what it was immediately as the name formed in my head. "You saw a Berkeley!" I exclaimed. Now I had never before seen a Berkeley and only knew about the existence of that obscure marque from hours spent reading and re-reading every book the library had about foreign cars.

The next evening an expedition was raised to investigate the little roadster. Sure enough, it was a Berkeley. A 1959 with four wheels (they made a lot of three-wheel Berkeleys) and a 328cc Excelsior two-cylinder motorcycle engine driving the front wheels through a chain. It didn't run, but this was one weird old car that I wasn't about to let get away. The owner looked like he came from central casting at a Grateful Dead concert. After some protracted financial negotiations, he took my $150 and one of my short-wave radio sets (a hobby that was quickly pushed to the background by the prospects of owning an actual motorcar). We hooked up a rope and flat-towed the little beast home.

Now that I owned a proper British sports car, albeit perhaps the smallest one ever made, and one that was not presently running, I discovered the joys of parts-chasing. Except, as my Berkeley engine came from a bike, I spent a lot of time hanging out in Harley shops, trying to match ignition parts from the Excelsior to something made in Milwaukee. One shop in particular had a field behind it that was a graveyard for old motorcycles. At the very back of the field, against a chain link fence, was an old gold-painted sports car. It was weathered but complete and I would glance at it as I scurried from cycle to cycle looking for parts that matched those from my Berkeley. One day the old gold car was gone. I asked the owner what had happened to it. "Somebody asked us about it so we gave it to him," was his casual response. I now know that old gold sports car was a rare Elva Courier, a car that today I would dearly love to own as a vintage racer.

Another wonderful racer would have been the Crosley special I saw one day for sale in front of a radiator shop. It was a single-seater, polished bare aluminum and covered with dash plaques from hill-climb events all over the Northeast. I didn't ask. I should have, but I didn't. I don't know how it got there, and sometimes I wonder if it still exists or if I will see it some day at a vintage race.

While in engineering school in upstate New York, I saw a lot of cars, but the ravages of road salt made the prospect of an old car much less desirable than it had been in balmy Florida. Most of the cars needed hundreds of hours of body work. I hate body work. I still looked, there was just less to see. Happily, my first job took me to rust-free South Carolina and any drive in the country could easily turn into a car hunting excursion. For a while some of us even formed a sports car support group. You could call its members anytime day or night and have them try and talk you out of a purchase.

Have I learned anything from these and many other chance encounters? Most emphatically, yes. I have learned that you should always and without fail, ask. At worst they will say no, or maybe the price will be more than you want to spend. But you never know until you ask.

Things changed a bit after moving back to the rust-belt in Michigan. The cars I liked, the sports cars from my youth, had rusted completely away or, worse, had suddenly become collector cars that bring many times their original prices. I fear the day of the $500 sports car has ended. But I still look behind old barns and garages as I drive through rural areas. Hey, it's better than complaining about the one that got away.

CHAPTER 26

Hooked on Speed:
From the ridiculous to the more ridiculous

I ran in my first marathon. I averaged right around 5-mph for the 26.2-mile course. The fast-guy elite runners covered the same course at an average speed of more than 11-mph. The quasi-religious experience of running that far has no doubt reduced the amount of oxygen reaching my brain, because it left me pondering the human race and this fascination we have with traveling the maximum distance we can over the minimum time possible. We begin life counting on others to carry us from place to place, but as soon as we are able we want to go faster. At first we use our own muscle power as we begin to crawl, walk and run. Next we use simple machines as we ride a tricycle and then a bicycle. Finally we harness chemical energy to propel us by driving a car and traveling by airplane. At each stage we up the ante of speed. Some of us seem to have a greater need to go fast than others do. Some of us seek out ways and machines that allow us to indulge that passion.

Take a Hike

Go for a walk. If you are in reasonable health you can easily walk 3-mph, although that seems kind of slow in a world that is so fast-paced. Okay, so start running. Over a short distance in a sprint, and assuming you aren't a super-human elite athlete, you can probably attain 8 or 9-mph. Elite athletes can reach as high as 14-mph. Doesn't seem very fast? I used to do a fair amount of sailboat racing and in that sport we would kill for a steady 9-mph, especially if the competition was only able to sail at 7-mph. The fastest I ever sailed in a mono-hull sailboat was a breathtaking 20-mph on a California-designed high-tech mini-sled called an Express 27. The wind was just right, the crew was on form and the boat leapt through the water, vibrating and singing as we powered past the fleet. Speed on the water is deceptive, as anyone who has ever had a ride in a ski-boat can confirm. A speed of 30-mph feels like 60-mph over the water and 60-mph feels like you're flying.

Man and the Machine

On the other hand, 20-mph is a pretty good clip if you're riding a bicycle. The idea of using a relatively simple machine to exchange muscle power for speed really took off at the end of the 1800's, as bicycles were all the rage. Until then, people were used to using animal power with horses, mules and oxen, or riding the rails using steam to propel them. Steam locomotives had been under development for nearly a century, chemically converting wood or coal into heat that could be used to generate steam. Steam was allowed to expand within a closed cylinder, pushing out a piston which, acting on a crankshaft, would propel the locomotive forward. Imagine the sense of velocity passengers must have felt at 40-mph on a train if they had never before gone faster than 15-mph in a horse-drawn wagon.

Enter the Automobile

It didn't take long after the invention of the automobile in the 1880's before daredevil racers tried to make them go faster. Jenatzy pushed the ultimate speed record to 65-mph in 1899 in his electrically powered car called *Jamais Content*. Henry Ford found 91-mph in his Ford 999 in 1903. By 1906, Fred Marriot in a Stanley Steamer had gone 127-mph and, in 1919 Tommy Milton had pushed that to 156-mph in a Duesenberg. From there, 200-mph (Henry Seagrave 1927) then 300-mph (Malcolm Campbell in 1935) came in an astonishingly short time as technology was applied to the problem. Aside from these feats of daring-do, ordinary passenger cars were also becoming faster, as well as safer at higher speeds. In the twenties, a car was pretty near its limits at 35-mph. By the early thirties cars could travel at 45-50-mph without drama. By the early 1950s, as roads got better and engines larger, speeds of 70-mph were easy to see on American highways. Today, thanks to aerodynamics required for better fuel economy, and better engine efficiencies that reduce friction and create more power, even the most mundane grocery-getter sedan can probably hit 120-mph or more. Crowded highways and speed limits prevent us from traveling that fast, but the cars we take for granted are capable of speeds that were once the realm of land speed record cars. There are even a handful of exotic and not-so exotic sports cars, coupes, sedans and even sport utility vehicles that can exceed 150-mph. If you have ever driven that speed on the German Autobahns, for example, you know that 150-mph means that 220 feet are passing by every second and that you'd better be on top of your game if you're going to travel that quickly. To do so in our uncontrolled driving environment, surrounded by inattentive drivers, would be shear folly.

The Friendly Skies

Speed over land pales in comparison to speed through the air. It didn't take long after the invention of the airplane before speed became an important part of the equation. Today, even a modest propeller-driven craft will cruise at 150-mph and it doesn't have to stop for stoplights and traffic jams. Commercial jets travel at 400-mph or more and the Concorde can travel faster than the speed of sound at something over 760-mph. Unfortunately for us speed junkies, commercial airliners fly so high, the sensation of speed is lost and progress seems snail-like as the earth glides by many miles below your window seat. The exception being takeoffs. Most speed junkies will recognize the push of acceleration of a 737 as being one of the best in the business. Travel by jetliner over long distances is fast enough to create a significant non-sequitor in the mind. I once left Tokyo's Narita Airport at 1 p.m. on a Saturday afternoon and, thanks to crossing the International Dateline, arrived in Detroit's Metro Airport at 11:00 a.m. on the same Saturday morning. Regular travelers of the Concorde between Europe and the U.S. report the same disconcerting sense of having traveled back in time.

Not So Fast

The reality of air travel for short hops is that it isn't really very fast, when you factor in all the time needed to check in, pass through security, wait for the aircraft and then get routed through a hub terminal that may be hundreds of miles in the wrong direction from where you want to go. On a recent 3:00 p.m. direct flight from Columbus, Ohio to Detroit, Michigan I had to leave at 1:00 p.m. to get to the airport early enough for the security and check-in procedures. The flight left on-time at 3:00 p.m. and arrived in Detroit at 3:55 p.m. By the time we got to the gate it was 4:10 p.m. and then, after picking up my bag and getting to my rental car, it was after 5:00 p.m. I figure that I could have easily made the drive between Columbus and Detroit in about 3 hours, easily beating the 30-mph average speed the airlines offered me.

It's All Relative

But let's get back to the idea that some of us like speed for its own sake. I have been racing and testing cars of one sort or another for over twenty years. Some of them have been very quick, but most of them have been quite slow. Most of my racing cars have been vintage racers that are slower than the street car you have sitting in your driveway right now. I used to joke that my minivan tow vehicle was faster than the Austin Healey Bugeye racing car that I was campaigning at the time. Okay, it wasn't a joke. It was the truth. On another occasion I can remember racing at an all-comer's race at Road Atlanta. I was driving a Saab 93 two-stroke sedan with a top speed of maybe 85-mph. Looking in my mirror while steaming down the back straight, I saw two small dots and, an instant later, was passed on both sides by a pair of Lola T70 sports racers traveling perhaps 100-mph faster than I was. The sense of speed while next to these two lightning fast racers was very real as they blew by, leaving the poor little 93 rocking in their wake.

This sense of speed is just as real when you're racing with a car that is just as fast (or slow) as the one you're in. This brings to the uninitiated the question: "Why would you want to race a car that is so slow?" If you've never been on a racetrack before, let me try to explain. Driving around a track is an exercise in repetition. The idea is to do each lap exactly like the one before it and to do each lap as close to perfect as possible. It doesn't matter if you are in a Saab 93 or a Lola T70, the concept is the same. That means placing the car in exactly the same spot every time, braking and accelerating at exactly the same spot ...well, you get the idea. After a while, even in a fast car, the process becomes ingrained enough so that the speed is no longer an issue. But driving around a racetrack, even close to the limit, isn't racing. Racing involves adding a dozen or more other drivers to the mix, each one also trying to drive on a perfect line while at the same time trying to stay ahead of you. If the cars are fairly well-matched and everyone stays on their perfect line, nobody is going to pass anyone. The trick is to place your car in a position that will still allow you to make it through a corner, but at the same time will prevent the other guy from taking his perfect line through the bend. This is how you pass another car. Because your car is not on its perfect line, not on the arc you have traced time after time through the corner, you have to slow down enough to still make it through the corner, but not so much that the other driver will come out of the corner ahead of you. Suddenly, the speed you are traveling relative to the other car, although it may only be a few miles per hour, is very real and, frankly, very exciting. It doesn't really matter how fast your car is or where you are on the grid. Just as in sailboat racing it's the speed relative to the other racer that you're battling that's important. As long as you have another car to race with, this sense of speed becomes very real.

Inspiration

During my several months of training for the marathon, I became familiar with the work of a magazine columnist for *Runner's World* magazine named John Bingham. Bingham is known as "The Penguin" because he waddles along at a pace significantly slower than the elite athletes do. In many ways he represents the majority of the 5,000-plus runners who were at the event I competed in, who were just looking to finish the grueling race. Most of us were back-markers, but that still put us ahead of the 100,000 people who came out to watch, and the hundreds of millions who would never consider doing such a race. I get the same sense when I'm driving a slow racing car at the back of the grid. The effort just to be in the race is significantly greater than the difference in effort between the first and last places in the race. It is clear that marathon racing has the same ratio of efforts. John "The Penguin" Bingham has a quote that always brings me back to vintage racing and the years I have spent driving slow cars quickly at the back of many racing grids. These are the words that everyone who races old cars should remember and pass on to those who would like to indulge their passion for speed. Bingham says, "The miracle isn't that I finished... The miracle is that I had the courage to start." If you like cars and driving, and I assume you do, then you owe it to yourself to listen to The Penguin's words. Unless you actually have a chance to drive a racing car on a circuit with others, you haven't really experienced what speed is all about.

CHAPTER 27

Simply the Best:
Answering one of life's great questions

What's the best car? That's invariably the first question people ask when they find out you write about automobiles. These people want you to say it is a BMW or the latest Porsche or something even more exotic like a Ferrari or Lamborghini. Mercedes-Benz is always high on everyone's expectations list. Sometimes you have to look around at who is listening. You can be sure that any mention of a minivan, no matter how versatile and practical they are, will result in stares of disbelief - if not outright guffaws. Nobody likes minivans anymore, not even soccer-moms. If you are at a dinner party with sensitive non-car people, they will want you to go into a long dissertation about why sport utility vehicles are bad and why electric cars are the way to the future. I'm always so sad when I have to disappoint them. Yet the question has been posed and the asker is standing there, waiting for my answer. What *is* the best car?

First of all, the question seems a bit unfair. If you ask the question in 1900, or 1920, or 1960, you would get a different answer than you do today. Not because cars have gotten so much better (they have), but because each era had its own standouts and its own duds. Is it fair to compare the road-holding of the live front axle of a 1930's Alfa Romeo 8C2300 sports car with the double wishbone independent front suspension of a modern Honda Civic? Each era had its technology and people who knew how to take advantage of it. That's why the aforementioned Alfa Romeo is considered one of the best sports cars in its time, even though a lowly Civic would blow it into the weeds of any on-ramp today.

Even some of the earliest automobiles were amazingly sophisticated. In the early days, when racing really did improve the breed, Peugeot had a 16-valve double overhead cam engine that won the 500-mile race at Indianapolis in 1913. J. Walter Christie built front-wheel drive racers between 1904 and 1908, while White and Stanley Steamers provided effortless and silent steam power and set land-speed records in the same period. Gabriel Voisin built ungainly yet highly aerodynamic racers in the early 1920's, while Mercedes and Auto Union's rear-engine racing cars of the thirties overwhelmed the world with engine technologies that would soon find their way into the skies over Europe.

After the war, racers continued to lead the way with two-stage supercharging from BRM, fuel injection from Mercedes-Benz, disc brakes from Jaguar, turbo-charging from Porsche and, later, Renault and practical performance four-wheel drive from Audi. But, these are racing cars and a whole other subject in the mind of the person who asked the question about the best car.

Let's ignore the racers then and just consider production cars. Here again we run into a problem. Is a car that is way ahead of its time, like the Citroen Traction Avant necessarily a better car than one of its contemporaries that is reliable, easy to repair and performs adequately well? Then what about the Mini? Brilliant design, ground-breaking passenger packaging, proven performance on racing circuits and rally tracks around the world, extraordinarily popular across every age and demographic group, yet it never turned a profit for its parent company. Actually, history is full of cars like Duesenbergs,

Auburns, Bentleys and Cisitalias whose production eventually caused the demise of their parent companies. Can a car be ranked among the best ever if it runs its builders into the poorhouse?

By now the person who posed the original question has glazed-over eyes or, more likely, has escaped to find more punch or dip. Maybe I gave a bit too much historical perspective. The person asking the question probably meant to limit his or her timeframe to the present. Perhaps they really meant to ask, what is the best car available today? Except cars aren't simply cars anymore. Pickup trucks and sport utilities account for half of the new vehicle market. Sport utility vehicles in particular have replaced cars in many driveways and it would be unfair not to include them in an answer to the question. Besides, many of the newest vehicles begin to defy description. Chrysler calls the PT Cruiser a light truck and both Subaru and BMW build all-wheel drive station wagons and call them sport utility vehicles.

And then there are the sports cars. The Miata remains an all-time great. The BMW M-Coupe is a strangely lovable throwback to an earlier age of motoring. The Honda S2000 is a twitchy little sweetheart that only rewards you if you always drive at the limit. The Boxster delights on a sunny afternoon on a twisty road. The Ferrari 360 Modena F1 is maybe the purest manifestation of performance you could ever have on the street. The Porsche Carrera 4 is possibly the most competent car on the planet if you are rushing from A to B on a rainy night. Still, if you have to take six people and a pile of luggage, it's hard to beat that minivan.

In fact, the reason the answer is so difficult is because there are so many great vehicles to choose from. Want a vehicle that will take you through mud bogs and over mountainsides, yet still will have the parking valets jumping? Take a Range Rover. Want a coupe that is obscenely fast, extraordinarily easy to drive, yet blends into the urban background? How about a Mercedes-Benz CL coupe? Think that's too German? How about a Volvo C70? Want more warmth than the Swedes provide? Jaguar's products are on a roll. Need to carry lots of stuff but don't want a truck? You can choose station wagons from Audi, BMW, Mercedes-Benz, Saab, Volkswagen and Volvo and that's just the offerings from the Europeans.

Any of those cars could be considered the best cars of today, depending on what you need from a car. Yet, deep inside, you just know that a list of cars for every purpose isn't what the person who asked the original question wanted. They wanted one: a single car that is simply the best; one car that you could proclaim head and shoulders above the crowd. I have always wanted to choose a Ferrari for that role. But they are so frivolous, so expensive. More like a toy than a car. How could I choose something so irrelevant?

Then, I drove the car that I could use to answer the question. The BMW M5 has 400 horsepower. It comfortably seats five in leather-lined splendor. It is quiet and serene and handles well enough to leave everything but a well-driven Porsche or Ferrari behind. Did I mention it has 400 horsepower? Its traction and dynamic stability controls can be switched off for evil, smile-inducing power slides. Its sound system is equally happy blasting out Mozart as it is with Smashing Pumpkins. Oh, and it has 400 horsepower.

The first party I attended after I drove the BMW M5, I was primed and ready for someone to ask the question. Finally, after years of boring guests with tedious explanations and thoughtful discourse, I had a single choice that would appeal to the snobs (it is a BMW after all), the enthusiasts (it is built by MPower, after all) and maybe even the non-car folks (it is a four-door after all). And so it happened. I was introduced to a polite-looking thirty-something professional. My host mumbled something about his liking cars and that I wrote about them for some magazine. His first question was the one I expected.

"So what is the best car?" I could barely contain myself as I blurted out "The new BMW M5 is simply the best!" He looked at me sadly and said, "Really? I would have thought you might have chosen a Ferrari…"

CHAPTER 28

This Could Work

I've pontificated upon the failure of modern racing to live up to its promise of improving the cars we drive. I called for a worldwide racing series that would not just provide entertainment, but that would help solve some of the problems that face our world. Several people (some of whom are even my friends) reminded me that while it is easy to find problems, finding answers is usually quite difficult. I have to admit that, as I wrote those words, I didn't have a clue how racing could be a part of the solution. Recently, while doing some historical research into the English Morris Motors Ltd of the twenties, I came upon a solution that is so outlandish it might just work.

Seventy years ago, Morris wanted a way of publicizing the performance and economy of their new Minor model. They devised a publicity stunt where a modified Morris Minor would cover 100 miles in one hour on a test track. The same car would also be driven 100 miles on a gallon of gasoline. Ok, so the company fudged the program a bit by changing from a supercharged racing engine in the performance test to a miserly economy powerplant for the economy run. The point was that both engines were based upon the production car. The car carried a wind-cheating single seat body to ensure that both goals would be met, and they were. Morris apparently made considerable hay from this activity and the pre-war Minor was a reasonable success.

It hit me like a thunderbolt. Why not create a competition with exactly the same goals? Imagine a car that will travel 100-mph while also delivering a hundred miles to a gallon of gasoline. Impossible, you say? Well, the top economy champions, flimsy single cylinder creations only suitable for track use, regularly top 2,000 miles per gallon. I myself have achieved over 60-mpg in both the Volkswagen Lupo and the Honda Insight hybrid car. If pushed hard enough, both of these cars can hit at least 80-mph. Besides, if it were easy everybody could do it.

What I envision is a competition held, perhaps, once every year like the Indy 500. The cars will be required to have two seats and to have a specific volume of luggage space, say, the size of four grocery bags (paper, not plastic). As much as I like old Morgans, we should probably require the cars to have four wheels - in the interests of maximum stability. Minimum weight should probably be in the 1000-1200 pound range. Wheelbase, width and overall height could be held to some reasonable size, too.

The running of the race will be familiar to devotees of sprint car racing. First of all, the cars would run on a paved oval. There would be four heats. In each heat each starter will be allowed to have the energy equivalent of one gallon of gasoline. If you have a diesel engine you get less than a gallon of diesel oil, as that fuel has more energy per unit volume. If yours is an electric car, you get to charge your car with the equivalent energy contained in a gallon of gasoline. The race begins from a standing start. In each heat, the top three finishers get to advance to the feature. Everyone else gets to run in a consolidation race and the top three will also make the feature race.

The trick here is that the person who goes the farthest in exactly one-hour before running out of fuel, is the winner. Imagine the race strategies. Think your car will go 100 miles at 100 miles per hour? Better get up to speed fast and stay there. Think your racer can go 60 miles in an hour on a gallon of fuel, but will only go 40 miles if you run flat out? Better pace yourself. Maybe one strategy will be to run hard. Go far and run out early, hoping the distance you have traveled will hold up and make you a winner. Add in the complications of accelerating away from a standing start and dealing with traffic and drafting, and the skills of racing will definitely be a major part of this game. But so will technology.

As new technologies are uncovered to make the cars go further and faster, additional rules may need to be added. Hybrids pose an interesting problem, for example. They get a gallon of gasoline in their tanks, but they also have energy stored in their batteries. Of course if we let them have their battery power, but then don't let them add anymore battery energy between heats, they will have to find creative ways to use the extra juice to their best advantage. If they use it too soon, they won't have anything left for the feature. If they hold back, they might not make the big show.

Cheating (or "creative interpretation of the rules" as it is called in racing) will obviously be a big part of this competition. This is not necessarily a bad thing. What we are looking for here is creativity and innovation in solving the basic problem of performance versus economy. Some teams will find ways of making their cars go farther and run faster and it is that kind of thinking that will have a positive effect on the future of the automobile.

The potential for involvement of tire companies, electronics manu-facturers and computer giants seems very clear. To get the most from a design will require new ways of thinking about how and where a car uses energy, and how to make it more efficient. The same disci-plines of aerodynamics and engine design that now pushes a racing car through the air at 200-mph, will be redirected into a more practi-cal problem of building a fuel-efficient automobile that can travel at more relevant speeds.

Once the series is established and speeds and economies have reached satisfyingly high levels, we can move on to road courses, where braking, cornering and accelerating will add a whole new dimension to the challenge. Crashworthiness and exhaust emissions are things we can worry about later.

Because racing today is more about entertainment than it is competition, we must think of that side of the equation. First of all, with speeds up to and over a 100 miles per hour, the cars won't be slow. Secondly, as drafting will be a big part of the game, racers will have to stay in close contact to gain any advantage. Whenever you have a group of cars traveling close together at high speed, you are going to have exciting racing. Inevitably, the best drivers will be the regular winners.

The real key will be to get car manufacturers to take such a challenge seriously. For too long they have been convinced by sanctioning bodies that racing's role is primarily entertainment. The idea that it could really improve the world, is all but inconceivable. What would be needed would be an appeal to the corporate ego, akin to the one that pushes BMW, Mercedes-Benz, Honda and Toyota to spend hundreds of millions of dollars in Formula One engine rivalries. It is possible, but it would require car makers to recall what racing really means.

When you boil it down to its essentials, racing has always been about managing energy to go as far and as fast as possible. Pits stops under caution and NASCAR yellow flags for debris often scramble this. But, in its essence, racing will always be thus. All I propose is that we limit the amount of energy to a pittance and make the goals as difficult to attain as possible. Racers have always shown an ability to overcome any obstacle and achieve the seemingly impossible. What I want is to, for once, give them a problem that is really worth solving. The future of the automobile.

CHAPTER 29

The future is in the Details:
Prognosticating what you will be driving

Ambrose Bierce once defined the future as, "That period of time in which our affairs prosper, our friends are true and our happiness is assured." Lately, there has been a lot of written word in the popular press about the future of the automobile. Much of it has followed Bierce's rosy prescription, describing in glowing terms the advances that are right around the corner: technologies that will allow nearly infinite fuel economy with less than zero emissions, in vehicles that drive themselves and are capable of transforming from lightning fast sports cars into roomy sport utility vehicles at the touch of a button. In other words, the best of everything for everyone. My only question: When has that ever worked before?

Predicting the future is a bit like playing the state lottery. You bet on your ability to correctly pick five numbers that are chosen at random. Even if you manage to get two numbers right, a batting average that any major leaguer would be thrilled with, you still lose. There is a reason that a bumper sticker calls the state lottery "A Tax on the Mathematically Impaired." Making predictions about the future isn't any easier. The random nature of events in the world makes any predictions, even fairly simple ones, far from a sure thing.

The answer from the point of view of the futurist then, is to avoid making any simple predictions. If you are going to be wrong anyway, you may as well grab some headlines in the process. Think big, in other words, and don't sweat the details. Unfortunately, it's the details that always seem to gum up the works. The obvious example for a car enthusiast is to point at all of those predictions in the 1950's that assured us that we would be driving nuclear-powered flying cars before the end of the 1980's. I still have a spot in my garage for one of those, but little details like cost, crowded airspace and the potential of daily disasters the size of Chernobyl seem to keep delaying progress.

For a while, the words "electric car" seemed to hold infinite fascination. That is until the details got in the way. Eventually it became clear that even the California Air Resources Board couldn't repeal the laws of physics. Batteries just can't hold enough of a charge to let everyone drive as casually as they do. Electric cars might work in a highly ordered and regimented society, the exact antithesis of what American drivers have always demanded and enjoyed. Without careful planning and discipline there is a good chance your limited-range electric vehicle will leave you at the side of the freeway, stranded and depleted. The idea was a good one, as long as you ignored the details.

At the tips of everyone's tongue today are fuel cells. The current common wisdom (which is much more common than it is wise) says that it's time to rip those nasty smelly gasoline guzzling internal combustion engines from the bowels of our vehicles and replace them with quiet, efficient, electricity-producing fuel cells that run on hydrogen we can get for free from seawater. On paper, fuel cells look great: combine some hydrogen and some oxygen in a space-age device, to create electricity and a little bit of water vapor. The electricity can be used to drive an electric motor to push a vehicle around. It seems simple enough but there are some fairly significant technical obstacles to overcome - such as cold weather performance, start-up times and cost. All of these pale, however, when compared to one seemingly minor detail: where will the hydrogen come from?

Hydrogen is the simplest and most abundant element in the universe. It is the stuff stars are made from and, with oxygen, one of the basic ingredients for water. It is also a byproduct for several fairly large industrial processes and can be liberated by electrolysis from seawater. The problem is that hydrogen is so light that storing a large amount of it takes either a huge amount of space, extremely high pressure, or an extremely cold environment. None of these three options are particularly attractive for a vehicle that has to eventually run across the ground. Most of the experimental fuel cell vehicles that have been shown by car manufacturers have used pressure vessels of cryogenically-stored liquid hydrogen. This is great for demonstration purposes, but manifestly impractical for a real hydrogen-powered vehicle. So it isn't just problems with fuel cells that need to be overcome. A whole system of production storage and distribution of hydrogen that has to be developed, or the fuel cell house of cards comes crashing down.

Meanwhile, some fairly clever engineers recognized that the hydrocarbon fuel called gasoline that powers our vehicles today are made up largely of hydrogen. Why not break up gasoline to get at the hydrogen and use it to power the fuel cells? Turns out this is easy to do in the laboratory, but terribly difficult to do in any realistic way in a vehicle. This is where the futurists come in. Since the concept is simple enough, even if it hasn't worked out on a practical vehicle, why not just claim that its just a matter of time before we are all driving around in fuel cell vehicles that use today's gasoline to produce the hydrogen that makes them go? Remember, think big and don't sweat the details.

It isn't just the engines that drive our vehicles that are the subject of prediction. Strangely enough, today's hottest predictions are about connecting people electronically, using "telematics." The idea is that people today are so connected electronically to their world that, when they step into a vehicle to become a driver, they can't afford to lose any amount of that accessibility. It doesn't take a futurist to recognize a world where your handheld phone/digital assistant automatically interfaces with your vehicle to provide telephone, e-mail and voice recognition so that you can be as productive on the road as you are in your office. If you are sharing the road with me, however, I would rather have you be just a tad less productive and a bit more attentive to the traffic around you.

But the futurists have an answer to my fears. These soothsayers find great appeal in vehicles that automatically drive themselves to any destination. Get in, sit down, tell your vehicle where you want to go and you are free to sit back and read or play video games while your fuel cell powered electric vehicle whisks you there safely and effortlessly. Even the most far-seeing futurist would realize this as a few years off. So, in the meantime, they point to recent demonstrations of experimental adaptive cruise control, video lane guidance systems and accident avoidance braking systems as right around the corner. Some of these driver aids do have validity in making the driving environment safer. They extend a driver's senses and provide more information about what lies ahead. When combined with dynamic stability systems and antilock brakes they can even help a driver avoid an accident. But there is a long way and more than just a few details between a system that provides a driver with additional information and augmented control, and a system that drives the car for you.

Fortunately, just as those flying cars were pretty far from the mark, so will "the future" be, as predicted by today's technological experts. If you compare an automobile of today with one from the fifties, you won't really see that much difference. Both are powered by internal combustion engines running on gasoline fuel. Sure, today's engines are cleaner, more efficient and much more reliable, but those are really just refinements of the basic designs. Drivers still use steering wheels to point a vehicle where they want it to go and press a gas or brake pedal to make it go and stop. Although minivans and sport utility vehicles have changed the external shape of the automobile, they are still being used in the same way that a station wagon would have been used by your parents and grandparents. There is a larger percentage of smaller cars around today, but Americans still drive big cars because that's what we need. The function hasn't changed because the transportation needs haven't changed. It is interesting to note that as the European middle class has become richer and less likely to use public transportation, their cars have grown in size and they have fully embraced the minivan and the sport utility vehicle.

So now I can add my curmudgeonly predictions to those of the futurists. If you are looking for dramatic change in the next ten years, you will be disappointed. The automobile industry is fundamentally a conservative one, and making wholesale changes is not a way to make steady profits. Automobiles are evolutionary, not revolutionary, products. While a ten-year old computer might not be fast enough to surf the web or run the latest software, a ten-year old automobile can make it back and forth to work or take you on a vacation without a problem. What's more, despite all of the optimistic claims to the contrary, new technologies like fuel cells are not yet ready for primetime and probably won't be before the end of the decade. It's important that car makers keep on doing the research and building vehicles that prove the concepts. Some are steps forward, others are steps back, but each tells us about what to try next. Except for a few such limited production experiments, in ten years the internal combustion engine will still be the powerplant of choice. Electronics will continue to provide refinements and aid to the driver, but if you are looking for a car that automatically takes you places, you will need to call a taxi. Unfortunately, unless something is done to curtail it, you will need all of those technologies that assist the driver because your attention will be diverted by answering your e-mail or making reservations at a sushi restaurant instead of driving your car. It's a good thing car makers have found a way to make cars safer in a collision. It looks like we may need it.

Henry Ford said, "History is more or less bunk. It's tradition. We don't want tradition. We want to live in the present and the only history that is worth a tinker's damn is the history we make today." Yet, if you want to know what tomorrow's vehicles will look like, I say you need to look at yesterday's cars. The needs of our society for mobility haven't changed that dramatically over the past fifty years and they won't change so very dramatically in the next ten. Our driving needs today are largely met by the same types of vehicles that were around thirty, forty or fifty years ago—when your parents were the age that you are now. The differences? They are really just in the details.

1952 MG TD

PARTS SUPPLIERS

Victoria British, LTD
P.O. Box 14991
Lenexa, KS 66285
(800) 225-0088
www.victoriabritish.com

Moss Motors
440 Rutherford St.
Goleta, CA 93117
1-800-667-7872
www.mossmotors.com

EAT FREE OR DIE

*From the outside, the life of an
automotive journalist seems like a dream.
From the inside, it could be murder.*

THE DEBUT NOVEL BY KEVIN CLEMENS

RELEASE DATE
Spring 2005

Copyright © 2004
By Kevin Clemens

The first glimmers of dawn were peaking over the sharp edge of the horizon. The Porsche's headlights illuminated several bleary-eyed people with towels and rags, wiping down the dust from the flanks of the other sleek sports cars. Behind them, standing on a ladder, a man peered into the viewfinder of a camera mounted on a large heavy-duty tripod.

"Move the Mercedes back about a foot," he commanded into the radio gripped in his ungloved left hand.

The car started and everyone paused and watched while the big black coupe inched backward.

"That's it, hold it right there," came the crackling voice over the radio.

The towel holders resumed their polishing.

Simon St. Scot stood at the base of the ladder and stamped his feet to get warm. He was glad he'd brought his beat-up brown leather jacket. He flipped the collar up against the cold as his breath condensed into a cloud.

Photographers were always pulling this kind of thing: up before dawn, drive forty miles out into the stinking desert to some rock formation that looked just like any of the other rock formations closer to town, then an hour of moving cars this way and that, until the rising sun provided enough light for shooting pictures; pictures that the magazine art director wouldn't like anyway, pictures that, in the end, would get manipulated with a computer, placing the cars into a seascape or a mountain scene.

St. Scot began to doubt if shooting sunrises and sunsets

was really necessary.

It was obscene to make everyone get up before dawn instead of sleeping in. They could have stayed out late the previous night and enjoyed a nice meal and a good bottle of wine at the magazine's expense. Instead, they'd cut the night short and now they were in the desert, at this ungodly hour of the morning, in search of the perfect shot. It was probably all a plot by photographers to exert their control over writers and magazine editors, Simon surmised. *Damn photographers.*

"Want to look?" asked Wayne Robbins, Simon's current tormentor.

Robbins must have been in a really good mood. Photographers almost never let you look. Simon waited for Robbins to come down the ladder before clambering up beside the camera.

The scene was dimly lit by the glow of the sun sitting just below the horizon, but Simon could see that Robbins knew his stuff. Arrayed in front of the lens were the Mercedes-Benz Coupe, a Ferrari, a Porsche and the new Jaguar sports car. Each was clearly visible in the frame along with some artistically arranged rocks and cacti in the edges of the composition. Simon scrambled down from the ladder and grunted something that sounded approving.

Moments later, Robbins was on top of the ladder checking his light meter. *Thwack-flap.* The sound of the Nikon's shutter opening and closing filled the still air as Robbins took the first of several hundred shots. Before the sun had fully appeared, the shoot was over.

As the senior staff person on this trip, it was Simon's unwritten and unspoken right to set the pace on the drive back to breakfast. Loafing along at 90-mph on the empty two-lane blacktop that stretched across the desert, he came to a long straight away. Glancing over to see where the other cars were, he fingered the paddle shifters on the back of the Ferrari's steering wheel, banged it down two gears and stood on the gas. The snarl of the V-8 rose to a frantic scream as the red car rocketed across the landscape. A flick of his index finger on the back of the steering wheel and the car banged up a gear. He watched smugly in his mirrors as Jopp in the Porsche and Wright in the Mercedes reacted to his charge. Robbins and Hayward in the Jaguar were last in line and, with the photographer driving, were left far behind by the sudden burst of acceleration.

As the speedometer crossed 140-mph, Simon eased up on the throttle and flicked the paddle shifter back into top gear. The other two cars began to close and he waited until they reached him, holding his speed for another mile or two before gradually slowing back to his 90-mph cruising speed. Nothing like an early morning high-speed blast in an exotic Italian car to put a smile on your face and the edge on your hunger for breakfast.

"You want hash browns, hon?"

Simon looked up into the inquiring face of Darlene, or at least that's what her Denny's nametag had written on it. He ordered hash browns, a three-egg mushroom omelet with rye toast, and a second glass of orange juice. It had been a good trip that would result in a cover story for the magazine. The cars were fabulous, the scenery was good (if you liked deserts), nothing had broken and nobody had crashed anything. That would make the new owners of the magazine happy.

Simon's job was to write about the Ferrari, the car he had gravitated to right from the start of the three-day drive. It was beautiful, of course, but it was also built by people who understood how to perfectly blend racing cars with a car for the street. It was poetry. It was art. It had intensity. It was like having sex with a supermodel...

His lustful thoughts were interrupted by Darlene, bringing their food to the table. She stopped and looked out across the window into the parking lot.

"Are those your cars?" she asked wide-eyed.

"Why yes, yes they are," answered Haywood. "Want me to take you for a ride?" he said, with something approaching a pathetic leer.

Darlene looked torn for a second and then deflected Haywood's opening with "My boyfriend has a Camaro and he would just die if he could see all of those cars."

The mushroom omelet on St. Scot's plate slowly soaked up the grease from the hash browns and he cut a piece of the artery putty with his fork and began eating.

It was clear that Haywood wasn't going to get anywhere. Darlene was cute enough: early twenties, thin blond hair and a slim figure in her Denny's outfit. She had a pretty smile. She had a very pretty smile. But what was Haywood thinking? They would be leaving in three hours. Ever since the guy had broken up with his girlfriend a few months earlier, he'd been hitting on every female he met. Women are good at sensing desperation. Haywood was several steps beyond that stage. Even Simon could see that.

Not that he was having much luck with romance himself. The problem was the job. The problem had always been and always would be the job. More than a dozen years earlier it had cost him his first marriage and, more recently, his second.

It was hard to build any sort of relationship when you were constantly flying off to Europe or Asia to drive fabulous cars and meet interesting people. Car companies flew you first class and put you in four-star hotels while wining and dining you at the world's most famous restaurants, but the travel was almost non-stop. Certainly it was a glamorous life and made you the envy of everyone at cocktail parties. It seemed rather petty to whine about it, but it was a lonely type of existence. Over the course of his career, Simon had been to some of the world's most romantic locales, mostly in the company of a dozen other guys. Some of his male colleagues found that situation intriguing, but it wasn't a lifestyle choice Simon wanted to embrace.

Sure, there were some women around, but female automotive writers were rare, and the ones who were part of the scene were savvy enough to avoid awkward entanglements with other writers. There were lots of women in the public relations departments of car companies, of course, but that would be a bit like sleeping with the enemy. His options were slim, and seemed to be getting slimmer.

Simon pulled himself out of his reverie, took out his corporate credit card and paid for the breakfast. Last night's hotel, a Four Season's of enormous charm and grace, had already gone onto the card and so should have a very nice meal in a well-reviewed local restaurant. Instead, Robbins had them out past ten o'clock shooting sunset pictures in the stinking desert.

Like most in his business, St. Scot fancied himself to be a gourmand and always looked forward to a really fine meal at a top restaurant, especially if (no not if, when) someone else was paying for it. But last night, like so many others on the road...*Damn photographers!*

As he signed for the check, Simon made a mental note to get his monthly expense report in early, since that Four Season's bill would hit his statement hard. His personal monthly record was $17,000, but that included a two-day rental of a Ferrari in Los Angeles for a special event the publisher had wanted to do. You could never get rich being an automotive journalist, but you sure could live like you were.

Simon hated being late for anything and particularly hated rushing to make a plane. Traveling with a laptop computer always meant even longer-than-usual delays going through security, so he liked to make sure he had plenty of time, even if it meant sitting around in the departure lounge or airline club. Robbins, on the other hand, prided himself on his ability to make airplanes by the narrowest of margins. The photographer had milked the time for some more shots for all it was worth and now the whole crew was dashing up to the ticket counter only to find that their flight had been delayed for at least a half an hour. Robbins looked at Simon smugly, as though he had once again cheated time and come out the winner.

Simon ignored him and, instead, pulled out his cell phone to check his voicemail. He hated cell phones and never left his turned on, much to the despair of the magazine's overworked Managing Editor, Mark Summers.

Summers was high-strung and nervous all the time and had the ability to make even the calmest people around him feel the same way. He lived in permanent fear that he was going to be fired at any moment. The nervousness was infectious and soon everyone figured Summers was about to get the axe. Even the upper management at the magazine would occasionally question why Summers was still around and why they hadn't fired him months ago. This caused nearly constant rumors among the staff that the Managing Editor was about to be fired, which, of course, fueled his anxiety even more.

Even though Summers made every kind of threat he could think of to Simon about leaving his phone on, Simon knew he didn't really have enough clout to make him change his evil cell-phone ignoring ways. Besides, he'd heard a rumor that Summers was about to be fired.

Simon checked his messages. Three calls from Summers asking him to call in as soon as he could. He ignored these. There was a call from Elizabeth Meyers. Meyers Communications was a major player with an automotive client who wanted to make sure there was a "car guy" in their PR firm. Simon knew that Elizabeth had more or less promised that she could get a senior editor from one of the big magazines to join her happy staff and she had set her sights on him. At first her flunkies had made the calls but now, because St. Scot hadn't been as willing to roll over for the dough, she was making the calls herself. She'd been trying to entice Simon away from his automotive journalism job and join the dark side of corporate public relations for some time now.

Many of his colleagues had already gone over and were pulling down salaries five times what they had as magazine writers. Almost to a person they had been changed by the switch, becoming corporate suits, leaving behind their reasoning power and their humanity. It paid a lot of money and all you really had to do was sell your soul.

St. Scot shuddered.

He listened to her message again.

They had once been, what?

Together?

No.

An item?

No.

Lovers?

Ah, yes, that was the word.

St. Scot figured Elizabeth Meyers would continue to court him to join her firm for another two weeks before she would give up on him and try to find another editor to coax to the dark side. He thought of the smell of her long silky auburn hair and the ample curves of her luscious body for several long seconds and then ignored her call, too.

The last call on Simon St. Scot's voicemail would change his life. It was from Blinsky.